The Idea of Florida

A Florida Sand Dollar Book

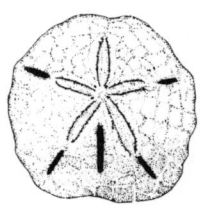

The Idea of Florida in the American Literary Imagination

Anne E. Rowe

University Press of Florida
Gainesville Tallahassee Tampa Boca Raton
Pensacola Orlando Miami Jacksonville

Copyright 1992 by the Board of Regents of the State of Florida
First printed in hardcover in 1986 by Louisiana State University Press
Printed in the U.S. on acid-free, recycled paper ∞
All Rights Reserved

Library of Congress Cataloging-in-Publication Data

Rowe, Anne E., 1945-
　The idea of Florida in the American literary imagination /
Anne E. Rowe. — Pbk. ed.
　　p.　cm. — (A Florida sand dollar book)
　Includes bibliographical references and index.
　ISBN 0-8130-1107-8 (alk. paper)
　　1. American literature—Florida—History and criticism.
　2. American literature—History and criticism.　3. Florida
in literature.　4. Tropics in literature.　5. Eden in literature.　I. Title.　II. Series.
　PS266.F6R69　1991
　810.9'32759—dc20　　　　　　　　　　　　　　　91-27085
　　　　　　　　　　　　　　　　　　　　　　　　　　CIP

University Press of Florida is the scholarly publishing agency for the
State University System of Florida, comprised of Florida A&M
University (Tallahassee), Florida Atlantic University (Boca Raton),
Florida International University (Miami), Florida State University
(Tallahassee), University of Central Florida (Orlando), University of
Florida (Gainesville), University of North Florida (Jacksonville),
University of South Florida (Tampa), University of West Florida
(Pensacola).

Order books from University Press of Florida, 15 NW 15th Street,
Gainesville, FL 32611.

All photographs are reproduced courtesy of the Florida State
Archives. Selections from *The Collected Poems of Wallace Stevens*,
copyright 1955, are quoted courtesy of Alfred A. Knopf, Inc.

To H. Lamar Rowe

Contents

Acknowledgments / xi

Abbreviations / xiii

Introduction / 1

I Vestiges of a Romantic Past / 11

II To Find the Phantom Pleasure / 26

III Vanity Fair in Full Blast / 44

IV The Garden Spot of God's Green Footstool / 77

V The Last Wild Country / 92

VI An Enchantment Slightly Sinister / 107

VII The Single Artificer of the World / 124

Epilogue / 137

Bibliography / 139

Index / 155

Photographs

following page 65

The bank of the St. Johns River

The *Osceola* steams up the Oklawaha River

Silver Springs

The Stowe family

Spanish-American War soldiers in their camp near Tampa

Fort San Marcos

The Breakers

The Ponce de Leon Hotel

Tea on the lawn at the Belleview Biltmore Hotel

A tea dance at the Royal Poinciana Hotel

Marjorie Kinnan Rawlings' home at Cross Creek

Ernest Hemingway's home in Key West

Acknowledgments

Many people helped me bring this work to completion. Thanks to my family, who encouraged me throughout the writing, and to the Department of English at Florida State University, which provided me with a supportive environment. Special thanks go to Nancy Chinn and Joe Wisdom, former graduate students in English at Florida State University, who provided invaluable library assistance. Daphne Williams Liedy helped me not only with her expert typing but also with perceptive editorial comments. I owe a great debt to Louis D. Rubin, Jr., who patiently read versions of this study and whose excellent advice and guidance kept me pointed in the right direction.

Abbreviations

AS	James, Henry. *The American Scene*. 1907; rpr. Bloomington, 1968.
CC	Rawlings, Marjorie Kinnan. *Cross Creek*. New York, 1942.
CP	Stevens, Wallace. *The Collected Poems of Wallace Stevens*. New York, 1955.
DDS	Cabell, James Branch. *The Devil's Own Dear Son: A Comedy of the Fatted Calf*. New York, 1949.
EA	Woolson, Constance Fenimore. *East Angels*. New York, 1886.
F	Lanier, Sidney. *Florida: Its Scenery, Climate, and History*. 1875; rpr. Gainesville, Fla., 1973.
GH	Lardner, Ring. "The Golden Honeymoon" in *How to Write Short Stories*. New York, 1924.
GS	King, Edward. *The Great South*. Edited by W. Magruder Duke and Robert R. Jones. 1875; rpr. Baton Rouge, 1972.
GT	Lardner, Ring. "Gullible's Travels" in *Gullible's Travels, Etc*. Chicago, 1965.

RF	Whitman, Albery A. *The Rape of Florida*. 1884; rpr. Miami, Fla., 1969.
SC	Lardner, Ring. "Sun Cured" in *Round Up: The Stories of Ring Lardner*. New York, 1929.
SJ	Cabell, Branch, and A. J. Hanna. *The St. Johns: A Parade of Diversities*. New York, 1943.
T	Van Doren, Mark, ed. *The Travels of William Bartram*. New York, 1928.
THHN	Hemingway, Ernest. *To Have and Have Not*. New York, 1937.
TP	Cabell, James Branch. *There Were Two Pirates: A Comedy of Division*. New York, 1946.

The Idea of Florida

Introduction

> How happily situated is this retired spot of earth. What an elysium it is! . . . Seduced by these sublime enchanting scenes of primitive nature and these visions of terrestrial happiness, I had rowed far away.
> —William Bartram, Travels

William Bartram, a naturalist, recorded many observations during his journeys in the South and particularly in Florida, which began when he accompanied his botanist father, John Bartram, on a plant-collecting expedition. He returned alone in 1773 to record what was intended to be a naturalist's descriptions of the flora and fauna, but they also became a paean to the beauty of nature he saw around him. The twofold nature of Bartram's *Travels*, published in 1791, has not gone unnoticed by critics; it has been cited as one of the earliest "artistic interpretations of the American continent. . . . The exotic landscape is not a background, but the subject." In his account of his journeys, Bartram uses a pattern of three parts: "withdrawal from society, encounter with wild nature, and return."[1]

At the outset of *Travels*, Bartram reveals that his work is not a laboratory look at nature. "This world, as a glorious apartment of the boundless palace of the sovereign Creator, is furnished with an infinite variety of animated scenes, inexpressibly beautiful and pleasing, equally free to the inspection and enjoyment of all his creatures" (T, 15). The naturalist is speaking here, and also the poet, who saw his surroundings as the manifestation of the Creator's glory.

In a sense, *Travels* depicts Bartram's retreat from urban life in the eighteenth century, for he was living in Philadelphia before his journey south. In April, 1773, he set sail for Charleston, South Carolina, in response to a request from his patron Dr. John Fothergill of London to explore the Floridas, as well as the western portions of Carolina and Georgia, "for the discovery of rare and useful productions of nature" (T, 29). *Travels* is divided into four sections, but only the second part deals extensively with Florida. Bartram's plan of travel was structured around journeys to the several trading stores that had been established in the territory, including the lower trading store on the St. Johns River and three more: one store sixty miles upriver (actually south of the upper store, since the river flows north); one fifty miles west at Alachua; and another west at Talahasochte, not far from Little St. Juan River, near Apalachi Bay, some 120 miles from the lower store. Bartram traveled to each of these stores and recorded his impressions of the terrain, the plant and animal life, and the Indians he encountered.

Among these several expeditions, however, it is Bartram's travels

[1] Patricia M. Medeiros, "Three Travelers: Carver, Bartram, and Woolman," in Everett Emerson (ed.), *American Literature, 1764–1789: The Revolutionary Years* (Madison, 1977), 202. Another fine study of Bartram in relation to the Edenic qualities of Florida is found in Elliot James Mackle, Jr., "The Eden of the South: Florida's Image in American Travel Literature and Painting, 1865–1900" (Ph.D. dissertation, Emory University, 1977).

alone on the St. Johns, from the lower trading post to the upper store, that epitomize the journey both away from civilization and toward the source of the river and primeval life itself. Alone on the river, Bartram finds himself in a paradisic setting in which his imagination soars, and there is a developing sense of his retreat away from worldly concerns into an idyllic existence. The physical retreat from civilization is paralleled by a sense of a journey into the past, for after going up the St. Johns and exploring the island at Lake George, Bartram concludes, "Our situation was like that of the primitive state of man, peaceable, contented and sociable" (T, 110).

Bartram was succumbing to the charms of Florida, and to such a degree that he did not allow the nuisances he found there to detract from the splendor of the setting. There were mosquitoes, but, though he mentions them, he minimizes their torturous stings. Alligators attacked Bartram's canoe, but he preferred to emphasize the amusement they provided with their nightly "barking." Bartram was less inclined to criticize than to make classical allusions when describing the birds and animals he saw, as when he writes of the snake bird. "I doubt not but if this bird had been an inhabitant of the Tiber in Ovid's days, it would have furnished him with a subject for some beautiful and entertaining metamorphoses" (T, 126).

Again and again, Bartram uses the word *Elysium* as he makes his solitary way into the wilderness. Referring to his expedition as "my sylvan pilgrimage," he comes finally to describe a night spent alone in the bosom of nature. "How harmonious and soothing is this native sylvan music now at still evening! inexpressibly tender are the responsive cooings of the innocent dove" (T, 140, 141). Elysium culminates at last in the garden imagery Bartram uses to describe his paradise. "This delightful spot, planted by nature, is almost an entire grove of Palms. . . . [It is a] blessed unviolated spot of earth. . . . A fascinating atmosphere surrounds this blissful garden" (T, 143). In this Eden, he finds, "every day's excursion present[s] new scenes of wonder and delight" (T, 203).

In his account of his travels Bartram captures the qualities of Florida that could so richly appeal to the imagination—the unspoiled terrain, the lush plant life and abundance and variety of animals, the breathtaking beauty of lakes and streams. As Bartram traveled up the St. Johns and away from civilization, he traveled closer to himself, to a place most harmonious to the inmost recesses of his soul.

For Bartram the retreat into the virgin wilderness of Florida afforded the opportunity to commune with nature in a pristine setting that offered unlimited potential. *Travels* is one of the earliest and fullest accounts of how Florida could touch the imagination of those who went there, and it embodies and is a precursor to what Florida would symbolize to the imagination of American writers who would treat it in their works.

A peninsula thrusting four hundred miles into semitropic seas from the temperate North American continent, Florida has been for the American imagination not merely a geographical region but an image, a garden, Eden-like, where the striving and seeking, the rigorous pioneering and getting ahead that characterize the Land of Opportunity has been tempered and diverted by the languors of a tropical climate washed by the Gulf Stream and the balm of an always warm sun. Just as the writer of northern Europe looked south toward a Mediterranean—*Kennst du das land* (where the citron blooms)—that offered surcease from the cares of struggle and survival, the American writer saw Florida as, in Wallace Stevens' words,

. . . a summer without end. . . .
Theatrical distances, bronze shadows heaped
On high horizons, mountainous atmospheres
Of sky and sea.[2]

Ralph Waldo Emerson, consumptive and seeking health, went to Florida from New England in the 1830s and found there a land far different from the country he knew. In Florida, he wrote, there was much

---

2 Wallace Stevens, "The Idea of Order at Key West," *The Collected Poems of Wallace Stevens* (New York, 1955), 129.

that can beguile the months of banishment
to the pale travellers whom Disease has sent
Hither for genial air from Northern homes.³

Harriet Beecher Stowe of Maine went to Mandarin on the St. Johns River in 1886. "Life itself is a pleasure when the sun shines warm . . . and I sit and dream and am happy and never want to go back north," she wrote back home. Stephen Crane arrived in 1896, looking for adventure, and set off from Jacksonville in a boat loaded with ammunition for Cuban insurgents, "loaded up as placidly as if she were going to carry oranges to New York instead of Remingtons to Cuba." Off the coast he found his adventure when the boat sank and he drifted for hours in a small dinghy almost within sight of land, as chronicled in "The Open Boat."⁴

Henry James, back home to see his native land after a long absence in England, journeyed to Palm Beach and St. Augustine in 1905, and was torn between his fascination with the physical charms of Florida, "the velvet air, the colour of the sea, the 'royal' palms, clustered here and there," and his sense of repugnance at the transformation of the resort areas into "Vanity Fair in full blast," great hotels filled with throngs of less-than-genteel pleasure-seekers.⁵

Ring Lardner, who regularly wintered in Florida after 1916, saw there both the seductive, alluring charms of the place and the ravishing of those same elements in the get-rich-quick land schemes flourishing in the 1920s.

In the 1930s, a century after Emerson had heeded the siren call of Florida, Ernest Hemingway, living in Key West after his return from

---

3 Ralph Waldo Emerson, "St. Augustine," in Edward Waldo Emerson and Waldo Emerson Forbes (eds.), *Journals of Ralph Waldo Emerson, with Annotations* (10 vols; Boston, 1909), II, 149–50.

4 Harriet Beecher Stowe to Annie Fields, 1872, quoted in Edward Wagenknecht, *Harriet Beecher Stowe: The Known and the Unknown* (New York, 1965), 81; Stephen Crane, "Stephen Crane's Own Story," in Fredson Bowers (ed.), *Reports of War* (Charlottesville, 1969), 85. Vol. IX of Bowers (ed.), *The Works of Stephen Crane*, 10 vols.

5 Henry James, *The American Scene* (1907; rpr. Bloomington, 1968), 449.

Europe, found in that semitropical place of sky and sea what he called "the last wild country," a place unlike any other in America where there were still the possibilities (though they were vanishing quickly) for a life unfettered, unencumbered by the increasingly rigid social and governmental institutions that characterized life in mainstream America. Wallace Stevens, who traveled to Florida on business, wrote home a response much like that of Harriet Beecher Stowe. "I have been down here actually for a week but it seems as if I had never been anywhere else and never particularly wanted to be anywhere else." In Stevens' poetry, Florida is the seductress who lingers on and on in the poet's memory.

> Donna, donna, dark
> . . . .
> Conceal yourself or disclose
> Fewest things to the lover[6]

Where the writers found images and visions, other Americans have found business opportunities, vacation resorts, retirement homes. With the coming of the railroad a huge influx of travelers and new residents went south, first to the Jacksonville area, then to Tampa and on to Miami, lining the beaches with hotels and condominiums. As a result, Florida today is vexed with the problems of a modern industrial society; and its 9.9 million citizens and its total bank assets ranking eighth in the nation constitute a vital and influential sector of American political and economic life. Still the idea of Florida persists. In spite of the state's assimilation into the mainstream of American life, the idea of Florida—the subtropical land, the idyllic, exotic paradise—continues to be a powerful seductive force.

Although probably not the first European to discover Florida, since both John Cabot and Amerigo Vespucci journeyed off the American coast in the final two or three years of the fifteenth cen-

---

6 Wallace Stevens to James A. Powers, February 19, 1930, in Holly Stevens (ed.), *Letters of Wallace Stevens* (New York, 1966), 258; Wallace Stevens, "O Florida, Venereal Soil," in Stevens, *Collected Poems*, 48.

tury, it is Ponce de León who has been given official recognition for the discovery of Florida. Juan Ponce de León was fifty years old when he obtained a patent from King Charles to search for the island of Bimini. His voyages and subsequent landing on the Florida coast in 1513 begin the official recorded history of Florida.[7]

His patent from the king gave Ponce de León power to govern the lands he discovered provided that he colonized them within three years. Thus, the reasons for his voyage were in part pragmatic ones. What has also been noted by historians, however, is that Ponce de León was likely aware of legends of rivers and springs in the New World, "of running water of such marvellous virtue, that the water thereof being drunk, perhaps with some diet, makes old men young again"—a fact not insignificant for a man already fifty years old when he set out on his journey. Ponce de León, comments one historian, "was convinced, as were all the other companions and successors of Columbus, that he ruled over islands spread out before that part of fabulous Asia which was principally known as a land of wonder and marvels. . . . As a geographical myth the Fountain of Youth is the most popular and characteristic expression of the emotions and expectations which agitated the conquerors of the New World."[8]

The enigmatic qualities of Florida would continue to fascinate explorers. Ponce de León had named his discovery the Land of Flowers, but it was also a land of swamps, mosquitoes, unpredictable weather, and hostile natives. The legends of the fountain of youth and the even stronger lure of gold continued to draw fortune seekers even though their hopes were not fulfilled. De Soto's expedition in Florida in 1539–1540 met with no success, for example, and he proceeded west in hope of finding gold there.

In 1562 Jean Ribault landed on the east coast of Florida, naming

7 J. E. Dovell, *Florida: Historic, Dramatic, Contemporary* (4 vols.; New York, 1952), I, 19 ff.

8 Leonardo Olschki, "Ponce de León's Fountain of Youth: History of a Geographical Myth," *Hispanic American Historical Review*, XXI (August, 1941), 363, 384–85.

the river he discovered there (which would later be called the St. Johns) the River of May in honor of the month in which he landed. Ribault's expedition, which was to stake a claim for France in the New World, was to lead finally to the bloody battle of Matanzas in which Ribault and many of his followers were beheaded by Pedro Menéndez of Spain, the founder of St. Augustine and one of the most powerful of the Spanish conquistadores.

The period of the first Spanish dominion, from the discovery by Ponce de León in 1513 until the treaty of 1763 when Florida was given over to England, was characterized by hope and disappointment, by stories of untold riches that lured a series of explorers who uniformly met with Indian attacks, disease, and a climate that offered no riches and little in the way of basic subsistence. The one published account of Florida by an Englishman, Jonathan Dickinson, who was shipwrecked off Florida in 1696 and made his way by land with family and others to Charles Town (later Charleston), depicts the territory as an unmitigated hell. As historian J. E. Dovell wryly notes, "That Spain held Florida for two centuries, despite enemy attacks, with but a few hundred men in the first century, and a few thousand men in the second century is evidence of strength of purpose, if little else."[9]

At the end of the Seven Years War, the treaty of 1763, in which the colonies of East and West Florida came under British rule, changed the direction of Florida history only slightly. It was during the period of British domination that John and William Bartram traveled in Florida, stopping at the Spalding stores that had been established on the St. Johns River. Immediately before the American Revolution about one hundred planters and farmers had established themselves in East Florida and loyalist refugees began moving into Florida from other colonies. Sympathy for the American cause was decidedly lacking in the Floridas, and in St. Augustine "information of the signing of the American Declaration of Independence . . . was

9 Dovell, *Florida*, I, 60.

received with such indignation that John Adams and John Hancock were burned in effigy in the plaza."[10]

Florida's association with England came to an end soon after the War of Independence. In the 1780s the Floridas were returned to Spain in exchange for England's right to keep Gibraltar. Both East and West Florida would remain under Spanish rule until 1821, when after forays by Andrew Jackson and his men to control hostile Indians, Spain took possession of west Texas and what would later become California, and the Floridas became a territory of the United States.

Some three hundred years after Florida's discovery by Ponce de León, the subtropical magic land, a land which in spite of shortcomings had maintained its alluring qualities, had become a part of the Protestant bourgeois United States of America. There it was: an untapped natural resource, an untapped imaginative resource, waiting for economic and spiritual (or imaginative) exploitation, much like Fitzgerald's breast of America that the Dutch sailors see. And it would be in the conflicting/complementary goals implied thereby (a land of enchantment/a rich land to be exploited or raped) that a drama would unfold that would elicit significant literary responses in the years to come.

The chapters that follow will examine the way in which the idea of Florida—the image of a tropical, lush "Good Place"—has been developed, explored, and interpreted by a series of American authors, beginning in the early national period and extending to the present day. This work is not a study of Florida writers or a history of Florida in literature. Instead it is an account of the way in which the idea of Florida has exercised and intrigued the American imagination as seen through the responses of the various writers who have come, seen, and commented—writers as diverse as Ring Lardner and Wallace Stevens, Ralph Waldo Emerson and James Branch Cabell, Henry James and Ernest Hemingway. They came, became enchanted

10 *Ibid.*, 86, 89.

with what they found, and then expressed their experience in poems, stories, and nonfiction. This study, then, is a study of an idea—the idea of Florida—and how it has developed and changed, but, nevertheless, persisted.

I
Vestiges of a Romantic Past

> Yet much is here
> That can beguile the months of
>   banishment
> To the pale travellers whom disease
>   hath sent
> Hither for genial air from Northern
>   homes.
> —Ralph Waldo Emerson
> "St. Augustine"

In the winter of 1827 a young man who had spent all twenty-three years of his life in the rigorous physical and moral climate of New England arrived by ship at St. Augustine, where he hoped to convalesce from the lung disease that was threatening his life. Ralph Waldo Emerson, graduate of Harvard, lately a schoolmaster, and only recently approbated as a Unitarian minister, brought all the preconceptions of his puritanical-transcendental-New England heritage with him to sleepy little St. Augustine, the oldest settlement by Europeans in America and only six years under American occupation.

The idea of Florida had not

immediately engaged Emerson. It is doubtful that he would have gone there on his own had not his physical condition required it. In fact, he had originally planned to recuperate in Charleston and had sailed there in the ship *Clematis* from Boston in November, 1826. Only after finding the weather in Charleston cold and dreary did he decide to go on to Florida. When he did arrive in St. Augustine he found the mild climate pleasing, but he was shocked by the indolence of the citizens and their lax attitudes about life, which were contrary to his New England ways. As one of Emerson's earlier biographers notes of his southern journey, "It was the first time he had ever been so far from home, and though he noted the increased grace of manners and the delicious air, at first his New England soul, nourished firmly on the belief in Purpose and the preciousness of Time, contracted like the sepals of a Calvinistic anemone at the sight of Southern laziness and slackness, accompanied by not a little dinginess and dirt."[1]

In spite of Emerson's misgivings, Florida evoked an imaginative response within him that grew from revulsion to ambivalence to what might even be called fascination. If the reality of St. Augustine included dirt and laxness, the soft breezes and the indolent way of life triumphed over Emerson's reservations. In both his letters and journals Emerson left a record of his response to Florida. In a letter to his brother William he remarked: "The air and sky of this ancient, fortified, delapidated sand-bank of a town are really delicious. . . . It is a queer place. There are eleven or twelve hundred people, and these are invalids, public officers, and Spaniards or rather Minorcans. . . . What is grown here? Oranges, on which no cultivation seems to be bestowed, beyond the sluggish attention of one or two negroes to each grove of five or six hundred trees." He reported that his amusement was to "stroll on the sea-beach and drive a green orange over the sand with a stick."[2] If indolence was not native to Emerson, he was at least able to adapt to it.

---

[1] Phillips Russell, *Emerson: The Wisest American* (New York, 1929), 63.

[2] James Elliot Cabot, *A Memoir of Ralph Waldo Emerson* (2 vols.; Boston, 1887), I, 121, 122.

In his journal Emerson recorded a poem entitled "St. Augustine," which captures his loneliness but also his growing response to the satisfaction of the little coastal town.

> Where peered, 'mid orange-groves and citron blooms,
> The little city of Saint Augustine.
> Slow slid the vessel to the fragrant shore,
> Loitering along Matanzas' sunny waves,
> And under Anastasia's verdant isle
> ....
> Oh, many a tragic story may be read,—
> Dim vestiges of a romantic past,
> Within the small peninsula of sand.
> Here is the old land of America
> And in this sea-girt nook, the infant steps,
> First foot-prints of that Genius giant-grown
> That daunts the nations with his power to-day.[3]

Significantly, Emerson moves the poem from the personal to the universal and alludes to the founding of St. Augustine by the Spanish as the first city in what would become the United States.

If Emerson shows the mythic qualities of the city in his closing lines, in a later poem he also reveals a bit of humor.

> Whilst here the fig and citron shed
> Their fragrant blooms
> And dulcimer mosquitoes in the woods
> Hum their sly secrets in unwilling ears
> Which, like all gossip, leave a smart behind.[4]

In these lines he refers to the same contrasts of beauty and discomfort that Bartram hinted at, but Emerson idealizes much less than his predecessor.

After wintering in St. Augustine, Emerson felt strong enough to return home, and in his journal he recorded a final tribute to the little city where he had regained his health. Here the New Englander finally succumbed to the charms of the place.

3 Emerson and Forbes (eds.), *Journals of Ralph Waldo Emerson*, II, 149–50.
4 *Ibid.*, 179.

There liest thou, little city of the deep,
And always hearest the unceasing sound
By day and night, in summer and in frost,
The roar of waters on thy coral shore.
But, softening southward in thy gentle clime,
Even the rude sea relents to clemency,
Feels the kind ray of that benignant sun
And pours warm billows up the beach of shells.
Farewell; and fair befall thee, gentle town.
The prayer of those who thank thee for their life,
The benison of those thy fragrant airs,
And simple hospitality hath blest,
Be to thee ever as the rich perfume
Of a good name, and pleasant memory![5]

Emerson left St. Augustine with his health restored; he was anxious to return home and begin in earnest his career as a scholar-writer. But the memory of St. Augustine was to stay with him, a brief languorous interlude in a life dedicated to thought and industry.

Another important result of his two-and-a-half-month stay in Florida was that Emerson met "his first superman in the flesh . . . in the person of Achille Murat." Murat was a nephew of Napoleon and the son of a cavalry leader who became marshal of France and king of Naples. In the nineteenth century, Achille Murat, as royalty in exile, brought a touch of glamour to the plantation he had settled on near Tallahassee. When Emerson left St. Augustine for Charleston, Murat was on board the ship, and the two men spent nine days in the same cabin discussing religion. As Jay B. Hubbell has noted, "In Murat, Emerson found what he had not believed to exist: 'a consistent atheist' and as ardent a lover of the truth as himself."[6] Emerson was taken with the young prince whom he saw as a much more dashing figure than himself, and their nine-day meeting of the minds

5 *Ibid.*, 181–82.
6 Regis Michaud, *Emerson: The Enraptured Yankee*, trans. George Boas (New York, 1930), 67; Jay B. Hubbell, *The South in American Literature: 1607–1900* (Durham, 1954), 377.

was to make a lasting impression on him. As late as 1870 there appeared in his essay "Society and Solitude" these lines that he had composed a decade or so before: "And if we recall the rare hours when we encountered the best persons, we *then found ourselves* [emphasis mine], and there first society seemed to exist. That was society, though in the transom of a brig or on the Florida Keys."[7] Although they were never to meet again and their later correspondence was not extensive, Emerson never forgot Achille Murat.

It would be foolish to consider Florida either as a major subject in Emerson's work or as a large part of his life. It is not too much to say, though, that Emerson was beguiled by the charms of Florida, that he went there hesitantly but left with happy memories and a written record of his days there which reveal that Florida struck a responsive chord in the young New Englander. Florida was a catalyst for the young man who before his journey south was in many senses a provincial, and he would not forget the lessons that he learned there.

When Emerson wintered in St. Augustine, Florida was only beginning to develop into a mecca for invalids from the northern states. With the introduction of steamboats in the 1820s, travel on inland waterways became more common and a greater part of Florida was opened to invalids, settlers, and tourists. By the 1860s paddle-wheel boats had routes on the St. Johns-Oklawaha, Suwannee, Apalachicola, and Choctawhatchee river systems.[8]

At the same time that the state was being opened up for exploration by the steam-powered boats, a series of battles were being waged in the territory that would determine the fate of the remaining Indians in Florida as well as dictate what would happen to the hitherto undeveloped lands. The confrontation would inspire a literary record of the Seminole wars that revealed the great disparity of attitudes toward the exploitation of Florida.

7 See John Q. Anderson, "Emerson and Prince Achille Murat," *Boston Public Library Quarterly*, X (1958), 27–37; Ralph Waldo Emerson, *Society and Solitude* (Cambridge, 1884), 17.
8 Dovell, *Florida*, I, 390–91.

Andrew Jackson had first entered the Florida territory to protect, as he put it, the settlers from Indians. The series of wars with the Seminoles, many of whom were the remnants of tribes that had been forced out of the older colonies, continued intermittently through 1859 and was "but a part of the general movement in the United States in the nineteenth century to push the red man farther west, though in Florida the movement was for long southward."[9]

William Pope DuVal, territorial governor of Florida from 1822 until 1834, and his successors found the conquering of the Indians no easy task. Loss of troops in Indian wars before 1838 was estimated to be up to three thousand men "all to subdue two thousand Indian warriors who had held out against an Army four or five times their number." A surgeon in the army reacted with disgust to a battle to oust the Seminoles from the edge of the Everglades: "It is in fact a most hideous region to live in; a perfect paradise for Indians, alligators, serpents, frogs, and every other kind of loathesome reptile. . . . Then why not . . . let the Indians have kept it?"[10] His opinion was not shared by most people, however, and by 1859 most of the Seminoles had been transported west and only a small number were left in the Everglades.

Two literary responses to the Indian wars, different from each other in almost every way, reflect the divergence of opinion about this period in Florida's history. Washington Irving and Albery Whitman had no firsthand experience of the wars, and their separate imaginative treatments illustrate how Florida could evoke a variety of responses.

Washington Irving, inspired by his reading of Bartram's *Travels*, describes the Seminoles of Florida as "leading a pleasant, indolent life, in a climate that required little shelter or clothing, and where the spontaneous fruits of the earth furnished subsistance without toil."[11] Although his knowledge of Florida was secondhand, gained

9 *Ibid.*, 235.
10 *Ibid.*, 250, 251.
11 Washington Irving, *Wolfert's Roost*, ed. Roberta Rosenberg (Boston, 1979), 184. Vol. XXVII of Richard Dilworth Rust (ed.), *The Complete Works of Washington Irving*.

from reading and from his friendship with William Pope DuVal, Irving's vision of this land was of a place peopled by a brave noble race who must ultimately confront an even stronger opponent in the American army. For Irving, Florida evoked visions of heroic struggles for a land that seemed every bit as exotic as any other place his travels had taken him, and certainly it was more intriguing than his own native New York.

Irving's interest both in Florida, the exotic tropic land, and his friendship with DuVal, the classic self-made hero, resulted finally in *Wolfert's Roost*, a dramatic account of the confrontation between two ways of life—that of the Indian in his pastoral setting and of the white settlers pushing onward, settling and developing more new land. For Irving, Florida, that lush, indolent place, must be finally "civilized" for the benefit of the white man. Irving's Florida, then, was a virgin territory ripe for conquest.

Irving first met DuVal in Philadelphia in 1833 and later published sketches of the fictional character Ralph Ringwood, modeled on DuVal, in the August and September, 1840, issues of *Knickerbocker*. *Wolfert's Roost*, a collection of nineteen sketches and essays published in 1855, contains two Florida sketches. "The Early Experiences of Ralph Ringwood" and parts of "The Seminoles" treat DuVal's boyhood, his rise to power, and, as governor of Florida, his removal of the Seminole Indians to the southern part of Florida.

Irving's second source for "The Seminoles" is William Bartram's *Travels*. Although Irving credits Bartram as a source, he quotes him much more extensively in his descriptions of Florida than he acknowledges. A recent source study indicates that though the opening and closing paragraphs of "The Seminoles" are original, the rest of the three-page sketch "is virtually copied from the *Travels*."[12]

Irving uses the Bartram material for several reasons. First, Irving apparently needed some supplementary material to flesh out his tale of DuVal. By incorporating Bartram's descriptions of his own encounter with the Seminoles in the late eighteenth century, Irving was able to provide some historical background to his tale of DuVal's

12 *Ibid.*, xxxii–xxxvi.

subsequent treaty for the removal of the Indians from north Florida. Even more important, however, is Irving's discovery of the exotic qualities of Bartram's description. Stanley Williams notes that Irving was almost "fifty years old when he was . . . subjected to the influence of the American frontier." It was then that "he discovered that a romantic might feed his emotions even in this America."[13] Perhaps one did not need to journey to Europe to capture the glamour contained in *Bracebridge Hall* or *The Sketch Book*. Possibly it might be found also in the vast outreaches of America. And that is precisely what Irving found in Bartram's work. Thus the appeal of such a passage as the following treating a young Seminole: "He was rather above the middle stature, and the most perfect human figure I ever saw; of an amiable, engaging countenance, air, and deportment; free and familiar in conversation, yet retaining a becoming gracefulness and dignity. We arose, took leave of them, and crossed a little vale covered with a charming green turf, already illuminated by the soft light of the full moon." And here the Seminoles were "delighting in bathing, passing much of their time under the shade of their trees, with heaps of oranges and other fine fruits for their refreshment; talking, laughing, dancing and sleeping. Every chief had a fan hanging to his side, made of feathers of the wild turkey, the beautiful pink-colored crane, or the scarlet flamingo. With this he would sit and fan himself with great stateliness, while the young people danced before him."[14] No wonder Irving hardly bothered to reword the passages; the material perfectly served his purposes.

Irving's second use of the Florida material is even more significant. His chance meeting with William Pope DuVal provided him with a wealth of tidbits that Irving, in his tales of Ralph Ringwood, was to recast into myth. As one source on the life of DuVal notes, "The little that is known of DuVal's life prior to 1800 is practically all obtained from the writings of Washington Irving."[15] In fact, when

13 Stanley T. Williams, *The Life of Washington Irving* (2 vols.; New York, 1935), II, 43-44, 45.
14 Irving, *Wolfert's Roost*, 184.
15 James Owen Knauss, "William Pope DuVal: Pioneer and State Builder," *Florida Historical Society Quarterly*, XI (January, 1933), 96.

DuVal became a Democratic candidate for the House of Representatives his opponents denigrated him as "a light-weight, made famous chiefly by Washington Irving's story of Ralph Ringwood" and claimed that "much of this story had its origins with Irving, not with DuVal."[16]

Irving's story of Ralph Ringwood is a classic tale of initiation. The young Ralph, angered by his punishment when he locks a mule in the family's smokehouse, sets out on foot from his Virginia home into the wilderness of Kentucky. Here the boy becomes a man, learning to live on his own in the forest and to kill bear and other game. Although he is befriended by a woodsman, he later decides that he must have an education, and he returns from the wilderness to read law. Irving also weaves into his story a courtship tale in which the young Ralph steals a kiss from a pretty girl sitting in a window and then later returns to woo and marry her. Ringwood then quickly rises to power.

In the Seminole sketch Irving returns to Ringwood, now referred to by his real name, DuVal. Selected in 1821 by President Monroe to be a United States judge for East Florida, DuVal was appointed the following year as the first civil governor of Florida. In the final section of "The Seminoles," entitled "The Conspiracy of Neamathla," Irving re-creates the confrontation of Governor DuVal with the Seminole chief. Here the culmination of the DuVal legend overpowers the idyllic depiction of the Indians as portrayed earlier by Bartram and adapted by Irving. When the chief Neamathla refuses to comply with a treaty and remove to a designated territory, DuVal rides into the Indian camp and is unswayed when the chief brandishes a long knife within an inch of his throat, vowing that "the country belonged to the red men, and that, sooner than give it up, his bones and the bones of his people should bleach upon its soil."[17]

Undaunted, DuVal replies: "You have made a treaty, yet you say your bones shall bleach before you comply with it. As sure as there is a sun in heaven, your bones *shall* bleach, if you do not fulfill every

16 Ibid., 136.
17 Irving, Wolfert's Roost, 187.

article of that treaty! I'll let you know that I am *first* here, and will see that you do your duty."[18] DuVal, through his show of strength, breaks the spirit of Neamathla and the Indians are subsequently removed.

In the concluding paragraphs of this sketch, Irving has finally enlarged DuVal to mythic proportions. The man who rose to power as a leader in Florida has single-handedly brought about the eviction of an entire race of people from his domain. Now this little spot of Eden has been "made safe" for the influx of white men who would come forth in even greater numbers to develop the state.

Although Florida provided for Irving an opportunity to seize upon the exotic qualities of this land for literary effect, and to write about a real-life hero, Irving's writing about Florida remains a minor part of his work. A more significant literary response to this period in Florida's history was that of Albery Whitman, a black writer whose poem *Twasinta's Seminoles, or the Rape of Florida* (1885) transformed the eviction of the Seminoles from Florida into an allegory of the pillaging of the New World. The defeat and displacement of the Seminoles from Florida was in many ways similar to the transportation and enslavement of the black man. For Whitman, Florida represented an unspoiled Eden which for centuries had resisted the fortune hunters of Europe. Now this land was finally being sacked, and by the very people who had come to America to establish a better world than the one left behind. Thus, Florida evoked for Whitman a vision of an idyllic land that, sadly, must succumb to the greed of fortune seekers.

When Whitman began publishing poetry in the 1870s and 1880s he was out of step in a literary sense. He was writing epic poetry at the height of the local-color period in which short fiction was a dominant literary genre. At a time when many popular writers were using fiction to heal the wounds of sectionalism, Whitman was reopening those wounds to remind his readers of social injustices

18 *Ibid.*, 188.

that had not been rectified. Richard Wright would later write that Whitman, having known slavery, war, and freedom, "spoke a tongue that denied him, belonged to a culture that rejected him, walked upon a soil that mocked him, and lived and labored among men who hated him."[19] Wright may have overstated his case, but Albery Whitman, born into slavery in Hart County, Kentucky, in 1851, would find himself a minority voice writing in an unpopular vein until his death in 1902.

Orphaned at twelve, Whitman attended school briefly at Troy, Ohio, and at Wilberforce University, where he became a protégé of Bishop Daniel A. Payne. He became an elder of the African Methodist Church, but on his own studied the poetry of Byron and Shelley. His lifework was the writing of several book-length poems including *Leelah Misled* (1873), *Not a Man and Yet a Man* (1877), *Twasinta's Seminoles, or the Rape of Florida* (1885), and *An Idyl of the South* (1901).[20] In the preface to one of his works, Whitman commented on his choice of the metrical verse form. "In essaying the 'stately verse,' *mastered* only by Spenser, Byron, and a very few other great poets, I may seem to have 'rushed in where angels fear to tread.' To this view of the matter, I will say by way of defense; some negro is sure to do everything that anyone else has ever done, and as none of that race have ever executed a poem in the 'stately' verse I simply *venture in*" (*RF*, 6). Venture in he did, but Whitman was forced to pay for the publication of his books himself and to promote their sales by reading from them before church groups.

What Albery Whitman was attempting to do was doomed to popular and commercial failure. As Joan Sherman in an essay on Whitman noted, "Born in the year of *Uncle Tom's Cabin*, Whitman repudiated Mrs. Stowe's stereotypes: 'The time has come when all 'Uncle Toms' and 'Topsies' ought to die. *Goody goodness* is a sort of man worship'."[21] At the same time that Harriet Stowe was in Man-

19 Richard Wright, *White Man, Listen!* (1957; rpr. Garden City, N.Y., 1964), 80.
20 See Louis D. Rubin, Jr. (ed.), *The Literary South* (New York, 1979), 400.
21 Joan R. Sherman, "Albery Allson Whitman: Poet of Beauty and Manliness," *College Language Association Journal*, XV (December, 1971), 128.

darin, Florida, penning reconciliation essays picturing good relations with the Negro, Whitman was writing poetry in which he used as his subject the plight of oppressed groups—the former slaves, the Indians, and all men of mixed races. Not only did Whitman insist upon reminding his readers (such as he had) that the Civil War had not magically solved all problems; he also rejected the only mode considered acceptable for black writers at that time—dialect poetry. At a time when local-color fiction and dialect both in fiction and in verse were enjoying great popularity, Albery Whitman was protesting in romantic verse. This is not to say that Whitman was always successful in the form he chose. As Sherman notes, his work is sometimes "burdened with overblown rhetoric and didactic digressions; however, he did supremely well with what he had: a sure dramatic sense, a talent for suspenseful narration, romantic description, communication of pathos, irony, and lovers' emotions, and the courage to attempt difficult meters and epic-length poems."[22]

Sherman notes that in his work Whitman looks "back to legendary pastoral worlds"—worlds that are being despoiled by greed and race prejudice.[23] *The Rape of Florida* bears out this analysis. The poem, some ninety-five pages long, narrates events of the Seminole Indian wars fought intermittently until the Indians were defeated and most were transported west.

Whitman saw in the plight and oppression of the Seminoles, who were joined by many runaway slaves, a metaphor for the exploitation of the black man who had been stolen from his native land and sold into slavery. In *The Rape of Florida* he pictures Florida before the entry of the white man as a lush Eden, inhabited by a noble race.

> Say, then, of that soon forgotten race
> That flourished once, but long has been obscure
> . . . .
> Say, when their flow'ry landscapes could allure,
> What peaceful seasons did to them return
> And how requited labour filled his golden urn!
> . . . .

22 *Ibid.*
23 *Ibid.*, 140.

How sweet their little fields of golden corn!
How pleasure smiled o'er all the varying scene!
How, 'mid her dewy murmurs dreamt the morn,
As Summer lingered in the deep serene! (*RF*, 8)

For centuries Florida was the paradisic home of the red man, but as Whitman notes, this land of pleasant groves and streams, the country Bartram had so much admired, was invaded, first by Spanish and then by French, English, and, finally, American conquerors.

Threatened in their paradise, the Seminoles responded heroically. The central characters in Whitman's poem, the noble warrior Atlassa, his beloved Ewald, and her father Palmecho, are heroes who with strength and courage rebel against the crushing forces of the army. Of Atlassa, Whitman writes,

Here begun
The valiant struggles of a forest son;
And tho' by wrong's leagued numbers overborne,
His deeds of love and valor for him won
The envied wreath by heroes only worn. (*RF*, 9)

Noble in spirit and body, daring enough to essay the rescue of Ewald's father from the fortress at St. Augustine, Atlassa and his companions are finally captured by the army and sent by ship to the West. At the conclusion of the epic, however, it is clear that here good has not triumphed over evil.

In his portrayal of the defeat of the noble Atlassa and his fellow Seminoles, Whitman makes several points. The band of Seminoles represent all conquered peoples who, making their life peacefully in their little world, are victimized by greedy invaders. With frequent references in his poem to the runaway slaves who often found friendship and shelter in the swamps of Florida, Whitman made his analogy between the two doomed races patently clear.

In doing so, Whitman also used his setting metaphorically.

Fair Florida! whose scenes could so enhance.
Could in the sweetness of the earth excel!
Wast thou the Seminole's inheritance?
Yea, it was thee he loved, and loved so well! (*RF*, 13)

In the poem Florida becomes a symbol for the garden of Eden, which is doomed by man's greed, and ultimately for the earth itself, which can never be free from man's rapaciousness.

> Oh! isn't the goal of life
> Where man has plenty and to man is fair?
> Where free from avarice's pinch and strife,
> Is earth not like the Eden-home of man and wife?
> . . . .
> If earth were freed from those who buy and sell,
> It soon were free from most, or *all* its ills;
> For that which makes it, most of all, a hell,
> Is what the stingy of purse of Fortune fills,
> The man who blesses and the man who kills,
> Oft have a kindred purpose after all,
> A purpose that will ring in Mammon's tills;
> And that has ne'er unheeded made a call,
> Since Eve and Adam trod the thistles of their Fall. (*RF*, 13)

Florida becomes finally for Whitman a symbol of America. In *The Rape of Florida* the virgin territory is cleared of her native inhabitants to make way for a more powerful race. The land is raped in the sense that a pastoral setting will now be exploited as hordes of greedy profit seekers pour in. Whitman could not foresee the building of the Gold Coast and the rise of the tourist trade that would be lamented and satirized by later writers such as Henry James, but he could mourn the passing of a pristine, lovely way of life. Lacking recognition in his own day, and, perhaps, coming short artistically of his own goals, Whitman nevertheless had the vision to use metaphorically a conquered race and conquered land and the audacity to make use of the "noble" verse to depict his race of heroes.

Although unlike any of the other writers who preceded him in his treatment of Florida, Whitman shares some common themes with them. Like Bartram he quickly sensed the Edenic qualities of Florida, sharing Bartram's sympathy for the Seminoles. While Irving created his legend of DuVal, the great white hero who finally helped rid Florida of the Indians, Whitman presented the contrasting picture. Like Irving, though, he used the same material to create heroes. Thus, Florida was able to provide legends from both sides. Clearly Whitman contrasted with his contemporary writers of the eighties and nineties in both his approach to Florida (revolutionary rather than reconciliation literature) and in his choice of genre, but like them he depicted Florida as that faraway country, a place rich both in legend and in physical beauty. In most ways unlike the other writers of Florida, Whitman still recognized and expressed its symbolic possibilities.

II
To Find the Phantom Pleasure

> *Pause with me at the gateway of the great peninsula, and reflect for a moment upon its history. Fact and fancy wander here hand in hand; the airy chronicles of the ancient fathers hover upon the confines of the impossible.*
> —Edward King
> The Great South

The Civil War had eclipsed for a time the importance of Florida in the American imagination. But though Florida was not in the mind of the nation, the state did play a significant if minor role in the war as a food supplier for the southern armies. Florida's location made it strategically insignificant in land battles, but the state did achieve the dubious distinction in the battle of Olustee in January, 1864, of suffering, on both sides, the greatest percentage of casualties of any Civil War battle. Although Confederate forces were victorious at Olustee, the battle had no influence on the outcome of the Civil War. Another Confederate victory in

To Find the Phantom Pleasure / 27

Florida, that of Natural Bridge, prevented the capture of Tallahassee, making it "the only Confederate capital east of the Mississippi" to resist capitulation to the Union army.¹

Although Florida did not suffer the pillaging and wholesale destruction that took place in other southern states, it was economically devastated by the end of the war. The plantation economy of the northern part of the state was in ruins, and the state's budding tourist industry had been temporarily squelched. At the end of the war, Florida's government was largely controlled by former Confederate supporters until military reconstruction went into effect in 1867. In spite of the lamentations of former supporters of the Confederacy, Florida during the Reconstruction period of the 1870s began an economic recovery. The state's reputation as a resort for tourists and invalids began to grow again, until eventually the Civil War seemed to have been only a brief setback to the phenomenal economic growth that tourism would bring to the state.

During Reconstruction, the waterways of Florida, which from the earliest periods of Spanish exploration had been major transportation arteries, were developed extensively as routes for travel and commerce. As Dovell notes, "The most publicized and patronized of the river trips from 1866 until the advent of World War I was the 'Silver Springs Tour' from Palatka to the Marion county springs over the Ocklawaha river and Silver Run." The development of the railroad systems in Florida also contributed greatly to the growth of tourism. Immediately before the Civil War there were about 400 miles of railroad in the state; by 1905 the number of miles had been increased to 3,500, in large part because of Henry Plant who built railroads across the state to the west coast, including Tampa, and Henry Flagler who began building railroad lines and hotels down the east coast, culminating in the overseas railroad to Key West in 1912.²

1 Dovell, *Florida*, I, 509, 515.
2 Dovell, *Florida*, II, 611–12, 613–17. For a perceptive discussion of the responses of Harriet Beecher Stowe, Sidney Lanier, and Edward King to Florida, see Mackle, "The Eden of the South."

If Florida captured the consciousness of the nation only sporadically in pre–Civil War days, the same would not be true after the conclusion of the war when reconciliation was on the mind of the nation. Florida offered too many things—an inviting climate, an exotic, faraway past, and the charm of quaint, out-of-the-way villages and their picturesque inhabitants—to be ignored by the rest of the country. And with the opening of the state through waterways and the railroad, the full discovery and exposure to exploitation of the exotic new wilderness was underway.

The charms of Florida made it ripe territory for sketches, articles, and stories, and one of the first writers to succumb to its attractions after the war was in many ways one of the most surprising. For among the loudest singers of Florida's praises was a woman who had been one of the harshest critics of the South. In a letter written in 1872, Harriet Beecher Stowe summed up what Florida meant to her. "I love to have a day of mere existence. Life itself is a pleasure when the sun shines warm and the lizards dart from all the shingles of the roof and the birds sing in so many notes and tones the yard reverberates—and I sit and dream and am happy and never want to go back north."[3]

That Harriet Stowe could write of Florida in glowing terms proves two things. First, Florida really was not like the rest of the South. Slavery had existed in Florida, but the highly developed plantation system of the tidewater and the Deep South had never made great inroads into the state. Harriet Stowe was not having to lavish her praises on a setting equivalent to the Kentucky plantation of *Uncle Tom's Cabin*. Second, and in another sense, Florida was like the rest of the South in its possession of the faraway, exotic qualities that appealed, perhaps on an unconscious level, to the population of the rapidly urbanizing Northeast. It has been demonstrated that Stowe, even when she was writing her harshest condemnation of the slave system, was nevertheless attracted to the genteel, idyllic

---

3 Harriet Beecher Stowe to Annie Fields, 1872, in Wagenknecht, *Harriet Beecher Stowe*, 81.

plantation settings, and, unknowingly perhaps, had continued in *Uncle Tom's Cabin* and *Dred* the pre–Civil War tradition of romanticizing the South.[4] The aristocratic southerners in both works are far more appealing than the northern characters; the slave owner Shelby, for example, receives much more sympathetic treatment than the northern-born Simon Legree.

A strong case can be made that even when her conscience directed her to criticize southern institutions, Stowe had difficulty in keeping under control her admiration for some of the South's more attractive and exotic qualities. Idyllic southern scenes and idealized southern characters continued to recur in her fiction. So it is no surprise that when the war was over, and the obligation to condemn southern shortcomings was removed, Stowe would overwhelmingly give in to the attractions of the South—especially Florida, a warm Edenic place where those southern qualities were even more intensified.

Stowe's capitulation came about when she began wintering in Florida after the war. In 1867 she rented a cotton plantation, Laurel Grove, to give a project to her son, Frederick, wounded in the war and searching for direction in his life; additionally, Stowe hoped to provide employment for a large number of black laborers. The failure of the experiment cost her ten thousand dollars, but convinced her that Florida was a perfect place to spend the winters. She purchased thirty acres at Mandarin on the St. Johns River, and from 1868 to 1884 she and her family regularly wintered there in a cottage among the orange trees.[5]

Soon she began writing sketches for northern magazines, becoming one of Florida's first promotional writers. In 1873 her published sketches of the people and customs of Florida were collected and published in book form as *Palmetto-Leaves*. Ranging from reports on the activities of the Freedman's Bureau to descriptions of picnics and boating parties, *Palmetto-Leaves* is long on praise and short on

---

4 Julia Collier Harris (ed.), *Joel Chandler Harris, Miscellaneous Literary, Political, and Social Writings* (Chapel Hill, 1931), 115, 116.
5 Mary B. Graff, *Mandarin on the St. Johns* (Gainesville, Fla., 1953), 44.

criticism. Even the burning of a bureau schoolhouse is passed off as the likely result of an accident.

As in her earlier writing, Stowe moralizes in *Palmetto-Leaves*, but here the emphasis is different. In the concluding chapter of *Palmetto-Leaves*, entitled "The Laborers of the South," she advises southerners to take advantage of the cheap black labor now available in the South. "The negro is the natural laborer of tropical regions. He is immensely strong; he thrives and flourishes physically under a temperature that exposes a white man to disease and death."[6] But this treatise of the economics of a black labor system is by no means a major concern in *Palmetto-Leaves*. The book's main purpose is to present the Edenic qualities of Florida; the beauty of the St. Johns River, the joys of a temperate winter, and the slow, indolent pace of life are the more important considerations.

Like many other northerners after the war, Harriet Stowe was tired—tired of the moral obligation to oppose slavery, tired of the fast pace of northern urban life, tired of the many responsibilities thrust on her in her role as spokeswoman for northern abolitionist sentiment. The indolent lifestyle afforded her in Mandarin, the time to just "sit and do nothing" was precisely what she wanted. Harriet Beecher Stowe was not unlike many other people whose fancies would also be captured by the promise of ease and relief from the pressures of everyday life.

While Harriet Stowe was enjoying the pleasures of life among the orange groves of Mandarin, a northern journalist was touring the southern states, recording his observations and sending reports back to the publishers of *Scribner's Monthly Magazine*. Although Edward King was not the first reporter to write of the postwar South, his treatment of it was much more sympathetic than those of reporters who went South immediately after the war and painted a grim picture of a still-rebellious people.[7] By 1873, when King made

6 Harriet Beecher Stowe, *Palmetto-Leaves* (Boston, 1873), 283.
7 Paul H. Buck, *The Road to Reunion, 1865–1900* (Boston, 1937), 16–20.

his journey southward, the mood of the nation was more one of curiosity than condemnation. Writing for an audience eager to be entertained and amused, anxious to be distracted with pictures of interesting people and places rather than preached to about social inequality, King had no trouble finding ample material in the South for his purposes. For Edward King, Florida was an unspoiled garden of delights. Yet as he praised its pristine beauty he also noted its possibilities for development.

King's collected edition entitled *The Great South*, published by Scribner's in 1875, resulted from the public's enthusiastic reception of his articles. A British edition was also published of this collection of descriptive passages, social commentary, and advice for economic progress. During his year-and-a-half stay in the South, King traveled more than twenty-five thousand miles in fourteen southern states. Although he was greatly concerned with the political and economic conditions of the states, a strong suit in *The Great South* is his colorful description of the southern landscape and its often-quaint inhabitants. Although King's work is nonfiction, its attention to the local scene and to the unique characteristics of the people who lived there closely aligns *The Great South* with the local-color fiction that was soon to dominate the literature of the 1880s and 1890s.

King was well into his southern tour before he reached Florida. He witnessed the Mardi Gras in New Orleans, journeyed by stage in Texas, and traveled throughout Missouri, Arkansas, Mississippi, Alabama, and Georgia before he made his way to Jacksonville, Florida, which he termed "the rendezvous for all travellers who intend to penetrate to the interior of the beautiful peninsula" (*GS*, 377).

King offered a brief historical account of the state before launching into a description of his Florida tour. Although his purpose was journalistic, the mystique of Florida captured his imagination in his historical sketch. "Fact and fancy wander here hand in hand. . . . what of fiction could exceed in romantic interest the history of this venerable State. . . . What 'fountain of youth' could be imagined more redolent of enchantment than the 'Silver Spring,' now annually visited by 50,000 tourists?" He continues, "Ceded and re-ceded, sacked and pillaged, languishing underdeveloped through a colonial existence of 200 years, shocked to its center by terrible Indian wars, and plunged into a war of secession at the moment when it was hoping for rest and stability, the lovely land seems indeed to have been the prey of a stern yet capricious fate" (*GS*, 378, 380).

Duty bound to give a statistical report on the development of agriculture and commerce, King launched into a sometimes tedious report of acreage, monetary value of products, and other economic concerns, but soon cut himself short. "We will not be too statistical. Imagine yourself transferred from the trying climate of the North or North-west into the gentle atmosphere of the Floridian peninsula. . . . Your face is fanned by the warm December breeze" (*GS*, 380). He makes a statement strikingly similar to Harriet Stowe's remarks in her letter. "This is the South, slumbrous, voluptuous, round and graceful. Here beauty peeps from every door-yard. Mere existence is pleasure; exertion is a bore" (*GS*, 380–81). Before he left Jacksonville to push further into the state, King noted that it is not only invalids who visit Florida. Only a quarter of Florida's visitors are seeking renewed health, "the others are crusading to find the phantom Pleasure" (*GS*, 382).

Making a journey by steamer up the St. Johns River before going to St. Augustine, King was enthralled with the foliage along the river's shore. "For its whole length of four hundred miles, it affords glimpses of perfect beauty" (*GS*, 384). He noted passing Harriet Stowe's home at Mandarin before giving himself up to the pleasures of St. Augustine. "During my stay . . . there were two days in which I gave myself completely up to the mere pleasure of existence. I seemed incapable of any effort; the strange fascination of the antiquated and remote fortress-town was upon me" (*GS*, 393–94). For the energetic King, as it had been some fifty years before for Emerson, it was impossible not to give way before the indolent pleasures of the town. Although the romantic in King feared that the "influx of Northern fashion" might rob St. Augustine of some of its charm, he predicted "a delightful watering-place is to be created" (*GS*, 396).

King also visited Palatka, where he found "Vermonters . . . in force," as well as the orange grove districts of the central regions. There the optimistic, enterprising King could not resist speculating, "We have within our boundaries a tropic land, rich and strange, which will one day be inhabited by thousands of fruit-growers, and where beautiful towns, and perhaps cities, will yet spring up" (*GS*, 400, 404).

King was most enchanted with his visit to Silver Springs. Traveling to the spring by steamer up the Oklawaha, a "remote and secluded stream, whose sylvan peace and perfect beauty will bring [the traveler] needed repose," he found it "one of the wonders of the world. The tradition that it is the 'Fountain of Youth' of which the aborigines spoke so enthusiastically to Ponce de Leon, seems firmly founded. The river or spring rises suddenly from the ground, and after running nine miles through foliage-shrouded banks, more luxuriantly beautiful than poet's wildest dream, empties into the Oclawaha. . . . We rowed about on the bosom of this fairy spring" (*GS*, 408, 412). Surely he had found paradise.

At the conclusion of his visit to Florida, King wrote of the St. Johns River that "the glamour of the Southern moon throws an enchantment over all the splendid foliage which makes it doubly bewitching" (*GS*, 416). Indeed, it seemed that King himself had been bewitched. The romantic history of St. Augustine and the beauty of the St. Johns and Silver Springs captivated the young journalist. *Scribner's* had commissioned him to write and popularize his views of the South; clearly, for King, Florida was the crown jewel among the many southern states he visited.

Less than two years after Edward King made his southern tour, a young poet retraced many of King's steps. His purpose for coming to Florida, however, was much different from his predecessor's. King was a journalist happy with his commission by *Scribner's* to make a reporting tour. Sidney Lanier was an aspiring poet and scholar, forced by poverty to accept an offer from the Great Atlantic Coastline Railroad Company to undertake what he feared would be hackwork. For Lanier, however, Florida afforded splendid possibilities for lyric descriptions. Although his assignment was to write a commercial tract, his pastoral vision of Florida transcended his mundane assignment.

Born in Macon, Georgia, in 1842, Lanier's plans for European study were cut short by the Civil War. Eventually he studied law, but the sixteen years he lived after the war were plagued with ill health and constant poverty. Although he could not support his family with his writing, he achieved a considerable reputation for the poetry and prose he wrote for periodicals. It was because of this magazine work that in 1875 the railroad offered him $125 per month and living expenses to make a three-month tour of Florida and write a guidebook to popularize the state.[8] Although Lanier was not optimistic about the literary possibilities of such a project, he was determined not to compromise his writing, and he would later refer to *Florida: Its Scenery, Climate, and History* as a "spiritualized guidebook" (F, xiii).

Lanier spent May and June traveling in Florida. The next three months he was in Baltimore, New York, and Philadelphia preparing the manuscript for publication. Lanier used a good deal of authorial license, changing the seasons of the places he visited, and occasionally relying on a secondary source for describing places he did not go (F, xxxv). Nevertheless the book is a penetrating, highly detailed account of his observations in Florida; for though he viewed the assignment as mundane, Lanier was too much a poet and lover of nature to fail to seize the opportunity to capture Florida's beauty in eloquent prose.

One example of Lanier's heightening for effect is the fact that,

---

[8] Jack DeBellis, *Sidney Lanier* (New York, 1972); Edd Winfield Parks, *Sidney Lanier: The Man, the Poet, the Critic* (Athens, 1968); Lena E. Jackson, "Sidney Lanier in Florida," *Florida Historical Society Quarterly*, XV (October, 1936), 118–24.

though he actually entered Florida at Jacksonville, he opens his work with a description of the beautiful Oklawaha River. Much as King had been enraptured by the small river, so was Lanier moved to praise it as

> the sweetest water-lane in the world, a lane which runs for more than a hundred and fifty miles of pure delight betwixt hedgerows of oaks and cypresses and palms and bays and magnolias and mosses and manifold vine growths, a lane clean to travel along for there is never a speck of dust in it save the blue dust and gold dust which the wind blows out of the flags and lilies, a lane which is as if a typical woods-stroll had taken shape and as if God had turned into water and trees the recollection of some meditative ramble through the lonely seclusions of His own soul. (F, 20)

As King had been before him, Lanier was struck with the beauty of Silver Springs into which the Oklawaha flows. He marveled at the clarity with which one could see sixty feet to the bottom of the spring. "It is as if depth itself—that subtle abstraction—had been compressed into a crystal lymph." As he glided over the spring, Lanier was enthralled by the color and light he saw around him. "The fundamental hues of the pool when at rest were distributed into innumerable kaleidoscopic flashes and brilliancies, the multitudes of fish became multitudes of animated gems, and the prismatic lights seemed actually to waver and play through their translucent bodies, until the whole spring, in a great blaze of sunlight, shone like an enormous fluid jewel that without decreasing forever lapsed away upward in successive exhalations of dissolving sheens and glittering colors" (F, 38).

Lanier devoted separate chapters to various parts of the state—St. Augustine, Jacksonville, the Gulf Coast, and other areas—with each chapter containing imagery that idealized the many wonders he recounts. The imagery is contrived the most, perhaps, in his description of the seasonal opening and closings of the Jacksonville hotels. "The Grand National and the St. James are open only during the winter; and when we came along back this way in the late spring we found rough planks barring their hospitalities up—a clear case, in fact, of roses shutting up and being buds again" (*F*, 69). To justify such a comparison, he adds, "This is Florida, and a simile will live vigorously in Florida which would perish outright in your cold, carping clime" (*F*, 70).

It is not surprising that in an account sketched in such superlatives Lanier would make large claims for the restorative powers of Florida's climate. "Consumptives are said to flourish in this climate; and there are many stories told of cadaverous persons coming here and turning out successful huntsmen and fishermen, of ruddy face and portentous appetite, after a few weeks" (*F*, 131).

The concluding chapters of *Florida* treat the region's climate and history. The temperature, writes Lanier, is "just cool enough to save a man from degenerating into a luxurious vegetable of laziness, and just warm enough to be nerve-quieting and tranquilizing" (*F*, 172). His treatment of Florida's history is nothing if not romantic. The state's first three hundred years were "but a bowl of blood" (*F*, 177). De Soto's wanderings he compares with those of Ulysses. Reflecting on the cruelties of the Spanish conquistadores and the brutalities of the several Indian wars he muses, "That such things could go on down among these green woods and streams—where any man in his senses must, one would think, be drawn by the very force of nature into large labors and peaceful dreams—is to me only another proof that the world has not nearly enough insane asylums" (*F*, 188). Lanier had begun his book with a picture of the beautiful Oklawaha. He closed his historical outline in a similar vein, musing on "the singular fate of this land which for three hundred and sixty years has languished, and has now burst into the world's regard as if it had but just opened like a long-closed magnolia-bud" (*F*, 208).

Florida: Its Scenery, Climate, and History is a guidebook, but it is much more than a superficial puffing for the tourist trade. With the single exception of the incongruous chapter "Advice to Consumptives," in which Lanier exhorts the curative powers of the area, his Florida book is a well-written account of Lanier's observations. It is far more organically sound than King's eclectic mixture of description, statistics, and advice. If Lanier at times overembellishes his imagery, the reader cannot feel that he is insincere, concerned only with the promotional purpose of the book. Far more likely, Lanier's deep love for nature, wrought to new levels by the lush Florida landscape, caused him occasionally to overwrite.

Lanier was to return to Florida a year later when he was dying of tuberculosis, and again the Florida setting would inspire him—this time to write poetry. Of this last visit one biographer writes: "He went out in the early morning on the shore at Fernandina, saddened not only with the poverty which had followed his every footstep, but now burdened by that darker enemy of disease, which was closing in upon the little remnant of vitality which was left him. The sun came up out of a calm ocean, flooded the back-lying marshes and live-oak forests with light and warmth and out of this morning of sorrow grew his wonderful poem of *Sunrise*."[9] He would write ten or so poems with a Florida setting, all of which sustained the earlier enchantment with Florida that he had felt on his first journey and had expressed in the guidebook.

Ultimately, Florida failed to produce the cure for Lanier that he had so optimistically described in his book, and the Florida book itself has not become a major part of the Lanier canon. If one remembers Lanier at all today it is for a few poems, "The Marshes of Glynn" among them, and a book, *The Science of English Verse*. But Lanier did produce a book rich in imagery, containing a valuable record of nineteenth-century life and travel in Florida. He lived up to his promise to himself to transcend hackwork and, as a result, left a small tribute to a place he had come to love.

At about the same time Lanier was in Florida in quest of financial security and good health, a popular writer of fiction was also visiting there. Free from the economic pressures that were driving Lanier, Constance Fenimore Woolson divided much of her time from 1873 to 1879 between the Carolinas and Florida. A writer of local-

---

9 Henry E. Harman, "Sidney Lanier—A Study," *South Atlantic Quarterly*, XIV (October, 1915), 303

color fiction, Woolson spent a good deal of time exploring the quaint and out-of-the-way places that provided the source material for her stories and sketches of provincial life popular with the readers of mass circulation magazines during the 1870s and 1880s. Woolson was attracted to Florida not only because of its warm climate, but also for what she perceived as its historical richness. In her Florida there is always a sense of the deep past against which her characters, usually drawn from contemporary life, act out their parts.

Born in 1840 in New Hampshire and educated in Cleveland and New York, Woolson did not go South until she was in her thirties. After the death of her father in 1869, Woolson and her mother traveled extensively throughout the eastern United States, often accompanied by Woolson's widowed sister, Clare Benedict. Woolson and Benedict studied guidebooks in order to prepare for their touring, which took them to New York, Philadelphia, Washington, Richmond, Charleston, Jacksonville, and Woolson's favorite place, St. Augustine.[10]

Woolson's southern experiences ended after her mother's death in 1879. She and Clare Benedict soon left for Europe where Woolson visited most of the European capitals and became an ardent admirer and friend of Henry James. She lived in England from 1890 to 1893, and died in Venice in 1894 after falling from her bedroom window. Speculation has never been put to rest over the cause of her death. The fall has been attributed both to delirium from influenza and to a suicide act resulting from depression. James worried that he had been in some way responsible for her death.[11]

Before she died Woolson had achieved recognition as a popular writer of fiction. Although her reputation has been eclipsed in the twentieth century, her works are finally being brought back into

10 For biographical details see John Dwight Kern, *Constance Fenimore Woolson: Literary Pioneer* (Philadelphia, 1934). See also Clare Benedict (ed.), *Constance Fenimore Woolson* (London, n.d.), and Rayburn S. Moore, *Constance F. Woolson* (New Haven, 1963).

11 Kern, *Constance Fenimore Woolson*, 161.

print today as representative works of the local-color period. Woolson's first popular success was her Lake Country sketches in 1875. Regional literature, coming into vogue as it did in the early 1870s, was satisfying a national demand on the part of readers in an increasingly urbanized nation to read of places untouched by the hustle-bustle of ordinary daily life. Woolson's sketches in *Castle Nowhere* (1875) of the Mackinac Island region where she had spent summers as a child, her Deep South stories collected in *Rodman the Keeper: Southern Sketches* (1880), and her novelette based in North Carolina mountains, *For the Major* (1883), were widely read. Like other writers of local-color fiction, Woolson's best efforts were usually short stories. Her quick sketches of quaint people and places succeeded where her attempts at extended plots and three-dimensional characterization in the novels were not as satisfactory. Nevertheless, Woolson published with much popular success four novels, each set at least partially in the South: *Anne* (1882), *East Angels* (1886), *Jupiter Lights* (1889), and *Horace Chase* (1894). Additionally, two collections of European travel stories were published by Harper and Brothers after her death.

Of the four novels, *East Angels*, the only one set in Florida, was her greatest critical success. Henry James gave it his characteristically qualified praise but pointed out real strengths in the novel, and William Dean Howells called one of the major characters, Edgarda Thorne, a triumph.[12] It is no coincidence that Woolson's best novel was set in Florida. She loved the St. Augustine area, which is the setting for *East Angels*. The mild climate and relaxed lifestyle combined with the romance of a deep historical past had quickly captured her imagination when she first visited there.

More important, however, the exotic qualities and indolent lifestyle that so appealed to Woolson at the same time seemed to prick at her New England, Puritan ethic of hard work and self-sacrifice. The working out of the conflict between indulgence and denial in

12 Moore, *Constance F. Woolson*, 98.

East Angels resulted in one of her most intriguing plots with two female characters who wonderfully epitomized the contrast between two opposing lifestyles.

East Angels follows the popular pattern of the North-South romance characteristic of postwar reconciliation fiction, with one slight twist. The North-South romance fails, not because Woolson did not wish to promote North-South reconciliation, but because for her purposes a North-South romance would ultimately violate her thematic intentions.

Woolson assembles her cast of characters in the little village of Gracias-á-Dios (St. Augustine), where Evert Winthrop, New Yorker and self-made millionaire, establishes his peevish aunt, Mrs. Rutherford, who is a "professional invalid." Winthrop falls in love with Garda Thorne, a beautiful young girl who lives with her widowed mother in the ancestral home of her father's family, a lovely if crumbling Spanish villa surrounded by an orange grove.

Garda Thorne epitomizes all the things Woolson and her readers found attractive in the South, and especially in Florida, "an existence which is not, for six months of the year, a combat" (*EA*, 3). Young and beautiful, poor but from an aristocratic background, Garda leads an indolent life doing little more than basking in the balmy air, occasionally eating oranges and allowing herself to be courted by various suitors.

In a practical sense, however, Garda clearly needs a husband who can give her the advantages her mother cannot afford. Evert Winthrop, a handsome, forceful man, seems the perfect suitor. But Woolson does not bring this typical North-South romance to its logical conclusion. Garda rejects Evert, and after marrying another young suitor and being widowed, is left to her own devices, leaving the reader with the impression that she will marry again but probably not successfully. By the conclusion of the novel it is also clear that as a result of another unhappy love affair which Woolson introduces into the novel, Evert Winthrop will live out his life unfulfilled by love.

The complicating factor in the story is Margaret Harold, the wife of Mrs. Rutherford's nephew and Evert's cousin by marriage. Deserted by her reckless husband, Margaret blames herself for the failure of her marriage. She comes to Gracias-á-Dios to recover from the separation and eventually falls in love with Winthrop. He returns her love, but she refuses to divorce her ne'er-do-well husband, becoming, in Henry James's words, a perfect example of self-immolation.[13] For Woolson, Margaret Harold's rejection of Evert, in spite of her love for him, makes her the ideal heroine, one who is strong enough to sacrifice all for honor's sake.

But the question of the abortive love affair between Evert and Garda Thorne is also intriguing. Garda embodies the qualities local-color writers were describing to evoke nostalgia in their urban reading audiences—qualities that were intriguing because of their elusiveness. Garda is of noble blood, living in an idyllic manner unique to her setting. She figures in the novel, then, as an ideal, a part of an Edenic way of life. Evert, representing the wealthy hard-driving industrial North, is attracted to Garda and what she represents. But, significantly, he cannot have her. One can be lured by a dream, but in Woolson's world, to possess the dream would be to destroy it; thus Evert cannot win Garda. Margaret Harold would have gladly married Evert had she been legally free; Garda, with seemingly every material thing to gain, turns him down.

Garda lives in a part of paradise. As her mother says, "Gracias-á-Dios *is* very far from New Bristol. . . . It's all the distance between a real place and an ideal one" (*EA*, 221). Representing the elusive beauty of an Edenic land, Garda becomes a symbol of an idealized existence, a hedonistic escape from reality. Evert Winthrop (and Constance Woolson) might be tempted by the escapist possibilities of such a place but could never give in to it.

In *East Angels* Garda becomes a symbol of what might have been, Evert of reality, and Margaret Harold of sacrifice and the rejection one must make of an escape from reality to a place dreamed of but never achieved. The character of Garda Thorne has been called a

---

13 Henry James, *Partial Portraits* (London, 1888), 189.

sort of "wish-fulfillment" for Constance Woolson.[14] But Woolson, through Evert Winthrop, ultimately rejected the siren's lure. It is well enough for Garda to luxuriate in the breezes and nibble tropical fruit; Constance Woolson had other work to do.

In *East Angels* Woolson did with Florida what had not been done before. Incorporating it in her fiction, she raised it to an imagistic and symbolic level never before reached. In her fiction appear the same beautiful images recorded in the prose nonfiction of Bartram and Lanier. Like these two writers she would glory in all the paradisic aspects of Florida; unlike them she would, through her characterization of Garda Thorne, explore Florida's symbolic possibilities. Florida here stands not only for physical beauty; it becomes representative of that Eden one dreams of in spite of the impossibility of achieving it.

East Angels is also important for another reason. The Edenic lure of Florida is unattainable here, but it is unattainable, perhaps, because it *must* be rejected. No case can be made for Constance Woolson as a writer who transcended the local-color genre. But in a significant way her work foreshadowed a twentieth-century love-hate affair with the symbolic qualities of Florida that would characterize the work of major writers, including Wallace Stevens. Woolson was able to focus simultaneously on both the glorious lure of the indolent life represented by Garda Thorne, and the spiritual deadening of such a way of life. Garda is beautiful but she is self-centered. Her life is gracious but it is also shallow. These contrasts were not considered by the earlier writers—Bartram and the others gloried in Florida. Bartram left Florida finally, but he did not reject it. The writer's relationship with the symbolic possibilities of Florida would become much more complex in the works of writers who followed Woolson. In *East Angels*, however, Woolson gives a hint of these complexities.

Stowe, King, Lanier, and Woolson each in his or her own way

14 Sybil B. Weir, "Southern Womanhood in the Novels of Constance Fenimore Woolson," *Mississippi Quarterly*, XXIX (1976), 567.

is representative of the dominant pattern of the treatment of the South, and of Florida, after the war. Each of these writers joined in the cause for reconciliation of the North and the South; each wrote optimistically of healing the old wounds inflicted by the war. The harshest critic of the South before the war, Stowe became the most vigorous promoter of idealizing literature of the postwar South. King, Lanier, and Woolson, in their idyllic pictures of Florida, followed suit, and through their writing the possibilities of Florida gained an even greater hold upon the American imagination.

III
Vanity Fair in Full Blast

> *In a ten-foot dingey one can get an idea of the resources of the sea in the line of waves that is not probable to the average experience, which is never at sea in a dingey.*
> —Stephen Crane
> "The Open Boat"

In November of 1896 a twenty-six-year-old American journalist-turned-novelist got off the train at Jacksonville looking for adventure. Stephen Crane had already written about the Civil War; *The Red Badge of Courage* had won him fame and fortune for its grippingly authentic depiction of the human animal in life-or-death combat, even though Crane himself had never been near a real battle. Now he was in search of an actual military engagement, and Florida seemed the obvious place to find it.

As the nineteenth century drew to a close, a variety of circumstances gave Florida a growing national visibility.

Florida's location at the southeast tip of the nation had kept the state from playing a central part in the Civil War. The same extremity of location, however, brought about Florida's involvement in the revolutionary activities in Cuba in the 1890s culminating in the Spanish-American War, in which Florida played a major role. The ties between Florida and Cuba were long-standing. Florida was not so many years out from under Spanish domination to forget its shared background with Cuba. Floridians had settled in Cuba when the Floridas were placed under English control in 1763; a similar emigration took place in 1821 when Florida again was removed from Spanish control and became a territory of the United States. Yet another link between Cuba and Florida came about later with the development of cigar factories in Tampa and Key West to which many Cubans went to work.[1]

Before the Civil War there had been a movement in the United States for annexation of Cuba. In the decades after the war a growing revolt against Spanish control was taking place in Cuba, resulting in the Ten Years' War, during which many Cubans left for the United States. Reports of atrocities by the Spanish toward Cubans in the 1870s and 1880s together with Spanish revocation in 1894 of Cuba's trade agreements with the United States for the purchase of sugar led to increased activity by the juntas, or committees of sympathizers, in the United States to provide financial support for Cuban revolutionaries.

In the 1890s the ports of Florida became chief operation centers for the filibustering activities which used steamers to supply munitions to the revolutionary forces in Cuba. One of these, *The Three Friends*, was owned in part by Napoleon B. Broward, who was to become governor of Florida in 1905. The explosion of the United States battleship *Maine* in February, 1898, in Havana harbor forced the McKinley administration into action, and war between the

---

[1] Two brief, useful discussions of Florida's role in the Spanish-American War include Dovell, *Florida*, II, 672–76 and Charlton W. Tebeau, *A History of Florida* (Rev. ed.; Coral Gables, Fla., 1980), 309–26.

United States and Spain was declared in April. The effect of the Spanish-American War on Florida was far-reaching. Tampa became the chief port for stationing and training troops before sending them to Cuba, and other camps were soon opened, including ones in Jacksonville and Lakeland. Key West's naval facilities were greatly improved. Along with the troops came war correspondents, including Richard Harding Davis, who were to send reports of the war to their respective papers. Although the war was short-lived—the troops arrived in May, the war was over in July, and the troops left Tampa by August—the soldiers and journalists went home with favorable reports of Florida. Tampa, along with Jacksonville and Key West, had achieved national prominence, and as one historian has noted, "the whole inglorious episode took place between two winter tourist seasons."[2]

Perhaps the best-known of the journalist-writers who went to Florida was Stephen Crane, who arrived in Jacksonville in mid-November, 1896, hoping to find a passage to Cuba in order to cover the war activities there. Crane had written about war in *The Red Badge of Courage*; he hoped now to experience it firsthand. In the four and a half months he spent in Jacksonville, Crane did not succeed in getting to Cuba; he did, however, undergo experiences that would have a profound effect on his personal life and that would provide material for some of his best work.

Although still a young man, only in his mid-twenties, when he first went to Florida, Stephen Crane was nearing the end of his life. He had jokingly predicted that he would die at thirty, and his prophecy would be more accurate than he had dreamed. By the time of his Jacksonville visit, Crane was well established in his career. Born in Newark, New Jersey, the fourteenth child of a minister, he had already had a less-than-successful college experience, had engaged in several unsuccessful love affairs, and had spent a poverty-marked period in New York City. More important, however, he had

2 Tebeau, *A History of Florida*, 326.

written and published some of his most significant work, notably *Maggie* and *The Red Badge of Courage*.

One of Crane's earliest biographers, Thomas Beer, in a brief reference to Crane's Florida experience called his stay in Jacksonville boring; however, William Randel has countered that judgment. "If Crane was bored and lonely in Jacksonville for more than a day or so, it was his own fault. The contemporary issues of the two local dailies, the *Florida Times-Union* and the *Florida Daily Citizen*, show that it was a very lively town, with unusual reasons for its liveliness."[3] A major source of interest and activity in Jacksonville in 1896 lay in the fact that the city was national headquarters for the Cuban Junta, organized to aid in the campaign to crush Spanish rule in Cuba. Centered in an office in a cigar store, the Junta sponsored filibustering expeditions, and certainly Crane was among those who hung on news from the Junta headquarters.

Not only was Jacksonville a center for war news, the city in the 1890s was still a major winter resort. The railroad lines had not yet opened the way for new resorts to be built in Palm Beach and Miami, although Jacksonville would soon be superceded by the development of the Gold Coast, it was still the major resort area when Crane arrived. In fact, the winter tourist season opened in November, precisely the time of Crane's arrival. For a young man who in his youth had written social items for a newspaper column on New Jersey summer resort life, there must have remained some curiosity about the winter social season in Jacksonville.[4]

Although one can only speculate on the extent of Crane's involvement with both the Junta activities and the social activities underway in Jacksonville's hotels, there are two events that took place during Crane's visit which had an indisputable effect upon him. In many ways tragic, one experience was, from a literary point of view,

[3] William Randel, "Stephen Crane's Jacksonville," *South Atlantic Quarterly*, LXII (Spring, 1963), 268.

[4] William Randel, "From Slate to Emerald Green: More Light on Crane's Jacksonville Visit," *Nineteenth-Century Fiction*, XIX (March, 1965), 358.

among the best things that ever happened to Crane. On New Year's Eve, 1896, Crane finally secured passage on a filibustering ship, the *Commodore*, bound south with arms for the Cuban revolution. The ship struck bottom as it made its way to the mouth of the St. Johns River, but only when it was out at sea and too far from shore to be helped was it discovered that extensive damage had been done. The ship was abandoned, and Crane was among those who survived in a lifeboat, which finally was brought to shore near Daytona Beach. Crane first wrote his experiences of the sinking of the *Commodore* for the newspaper. Immediately he set about reworking the material in short story form, producing what has been judged his best work of short fiction, "The Open Boat."[5]

The other important event in Crane's Jacksonville stay was certainly far less beneficial to his literary career though for a time at least it seemed to bring him happiness. Scholars have documented Crane's great sympathy for ladies of the night. In New York he had once jeopardized his public reputation by protesting the arrest of a young girl of the streets. Crane was not unfamiliar with houses of pleasure, and he did not avoid them in Jacksonville. Although Ward Street, or "the line" as it was called, had the most of these houses, the more "genteel" establishments were located elsewhere. The "best of all the houses in town" was owned by Cora Taylor, and its name, Hotel de Dreme, certainly reflected the aspirations of its proprietress.[6] Cora had already enjoyed a colorful life, having married and divorced an English nobleman who was disowned by his family, before settling in Jacksonville to open her house of entertainment, which was patronized by the "best" Jacksonville citizens. When the romantic Cora met Stephen Crane, however, she knew that she had found the love of her life, and Crane, who had unsuccessfully pursued more mature women before, returned her affection. When he left the United States in 1897 to become a war corre-

5 See J. C. Levenson, Introduction to Fredson Bowers (ed.), *Tales of Adventure* (Charlottesville, 1970), lviii–lxx. Vol. V of Bowers (ed.), *The Works of Stephen Crane*, 10 vols.

6 Randel, "Stephen Crane's Jacksonville," 270.

spondent in Greece, Cora followed him, becoming the first American woman war correspondent.

Crane indulged Cora's penchant for a lavish life-style. Although there is no official record that they married, Cora called herself Mrs. Stephen Crane and led Crane to Brede Manor in Sussex, England. In 1898, when Crane left Cora temporarily to cover the Spanish-American War in Cuba, she pursued him by telegram and mail, imploring him to return to Brede Manor. Before he returned, however, he had spent time in Cuba and again in Florida, this time in Tampa and Key West. The Florida experience was less significant on this journey, but it did provide material for a minor, but fascinating, story, "The Clan of No-Name." At last Cora prevailed, and driven by his sense of duty, Crane returned to England. The last years of Crane's life, when he was suffering from lung disease, were spent feverishly trying to write enough to support the high cost of estate living. Always one step ahead of the creditors, Cora was unable to curb their spending in those final years.

The writing of the last years was much inferior to such work as *Maggie* and "The Open Boat" and the other major pieces. Crane wrote in bed, up to the final days of his life. At twenty-eight he died in Germany where Cora had taken him in the vain hope of a cure. Cora's dreams died with Crane. After an unsuccessful attempt at supporting herself by writing, she returned to Jacksonville and opened another house, euphemistically named the Court.

Crane's use of his Florida experiences in his writing reflects the state's associations both with the war activities and with the growing tourist industry. His first use of the *Commodore* disaster, though superior in style, is much like the journalistic writing of his predecessor, Edward King. The newspaper account dated January 6, less than a week after the sinking of the ship, is a straightforward account of events from the time the ship left Jacksonville on New Year's Day until the rescue of the men in the lifeboat near Mosquito Inlet. Like King, Crane uses colorful language in his portrayal, as when he describes the loading of the boat. "Her hatch, like the mouth of a monster, engulfed [boxes of ammunition and bundles of rifles]. It might have been the feeding time of some legendary creature of the sea." The ship, he continues, "loaded up as placidly as if she were going to carry oranges to New York, instead of Remingtons to Cuba."[7]

Although Crane uses some fanciful language, the account remains strictly on the journalistic level, an eyewitness account by a participant. Although Crane lavished detail upon the loading of the *Commodore*, the striking bottom on the St. Johns River, and the journey out to sea, he curiously compressed the material that would later be used in his short story.

> The history of life in an open boat for thirty hours would no doubt be very instructive for the young, but none is to be told here now. For my part I would prefer to tell the story at once, because from it would shine the splendid manhood of Captain Edward Murphy and of William Higgins, the oiler, but let it suffice at this time to say that when we were swamped in the surf and making the best of our way toward the shore the captain gave orders amid the wildness of the breakers as clearly as if he had been on the quarterdeck of a battleship.[8]

Crane's account ends with only one additional paragraph, four sentences long, in which he describes Higgins' death and the rescue of Captain Murphy, the cook, and himself.

In this truncated report of the thirty hours in the open boat and the rescue is evidence that Crane knew at once that he had a story to tell. He would not waste his material in a newspaper article. What would follow was one of Crane's greatest stories, and the most technically and artistically superior work of literature set in Florida up to that time. With the publication of "The Open Boat," Florida would gain a place in the mainstream of American literature.

In his introduction to the story in the Virginia edition of *The*

---

7 Stephen Crane, "Stephen Crane's Own Story," in Fredson Bowers (ed.), *Reports of War* (Charlottesville, 1969), 85. Vol. IX of Bowers (ed.), *The Works of Stephen Crane*, 10 vols.

8 *Ibid.*, 94.

Works of Stephen Crane, J. C. Levenson notes that "Crane managed to fuse the most external and the most inward of narrative forms, the tale of adventure and the fiction of consciousness." Crane, accordingly, accomplishes in the story what he did not do in the earlier newspaper account. "The Open Boat" recounts the tale of the four men, but here Crane fuses the story line with the growth in understanding of the correspondent. As Levenson notes, "The expansion of consciousness leads at last to the encounter with that absolute finality, the extinction of consciousness. The progress from self-engrossment to clear vision, from fanciful outrage to puzzled acceptance, is a growth of moral intelligence which does not simply come from within. The encounter with reality has made a crucial difference."[9]

The point here, then, is that in "The Open Boat" the effect of the setting—here the Florida sea and shore—on the developing consciousness of the narrator is of central importance. It can be argued that this could be a shipwreck anywhere, at any time. But it is not anywhere; Crane carefully pinpoints the location off Mosquito Inlet, and he uses the hotel omnibus, so characteristic of resort life, as an ironic contrast to the plight of the men in the dinghy. Their condition becomes even more horrible when it becomes clear that the people on the shore fail to recognize their dangerous situation.

It is difficult to articulate what exactly the correspondent has learned, but it is certain that he has undergone a change, that from his thirty hours in the dinghy he has emerged a wiser man. As the three survivors step on shore, they are quickly surrounded by women bringing coffee, blankets, and other comforts. The men have reentered a world in which the threat of death seems far away, but for the correspondent and his companions the comforts offered on the beach at Daytona cannot erase the lessons learned from the sea.

Crane finished writing "The Open Boat" in February and by the following month had decided to leave Florida. His one filibustering experience had failed to get him to Cuba; he would try to observe

---

9 Levenson, Introduction to Bowers (ed.), *Tales of Adventure*, lxvi, lxviii.

the revolution in Crete. He was in New York for a week in March and during that time negotiated a deal with S. S. McClure for an advance loan in return for which he promised his next book; he started at once another Florida story, "Flanagan and His Short Filibustering Adventure."[10]

Although in "Flanagan" Crane drew upon the same experience he had used for "The Open Boat," the second Florida story is inferior in style and technique. The title derives from the name of the ship's master who is hired for a filibustering expedition. Crane recounts Flanagan's adventures as he evades first American patrols to load his ship, the *Foundling*, with arms and then Cuban patrols to unload the arms in Cuba. All goes successfully until, pursued by a Spanish gunboat, the *Foundling* turns at her pursuer and crashes against her. The seams of the boat are weakened by the blow, but parallel to the experience of the *Commodore*, the captain does not realize the extent of damage until the ship is out at sea.

In "Flanagan" Crane fashions his tale by selectively excluding what was included in "The Open Boat" and including what was omitted. Although the story is not a literal representation of the *Commodore* experience, the sinking of the *Foundling* closely parallels the loss of the *Commodore*. In "Flanagan," in contrast to "The Open Boat," the scene shifts entirely away from the men in the boat. "When finally the *Foundling* sank she shifted and settled as calmly as an animal curls down in the bush grass. Away over the waves two bobbing boats paused to witness quiet death." Watching her sink, "the captain whirled and knocked his head on the gunwale. He sobbed for a time, and then he sobbed and swore also."[11]

At this point in the story, Crane veers away from the shipwrecked men, and, in an intriguing shift in point of view, switches to the activities on shore. What follows is a fascinating contrast between the life-and-death situation of the men in the lifeboats and the social

10 Stephen Crane, "Flanagan and His Short Filibustering Career," in Bowers (ed.), *Tales of Adventure*, 93–108.
11 Ibid., 107.

scene at the coastal resort. Not only does the setting change; the narrative attitude shifts as well. "There was a dance at the Imperial Inn. During the evening some irresponsible young men came from the beach bringing the statement that several boatloads of people had been perceived off shore. It was a charming dance, and none cared to take time to believe this tale." [12]

Crane seems to satirize the selfish attitude of the revelers who do not want their fun spoiled by such an unpleasant occurrence as a shipwreck. Crane heightens his effect by emphasizing the dreamlike qualities of the setting. "The fountain in the courtyard plashed softly, and couple after couple paraded through the aisles of palms where lamps with red shades threw a rose light upon the gleaming leaves. High on some balcony a mocking-bird called into the evening. The band played its waltzes slumberously, and its music to the people among the palms came faintly and like the melodies in dreams." [13]

As the dance continues a woman occasionally queries that it couldn't really be true that there was a wreck at sea. And a man answers, "No, of course not." Finally, a youth comes suddenly from the beach and triumphantly reports that there is indeed a whole boatload of survivors out in the water. The narrator notes, "His news destroyed the dance." The dancers rush to the shore, the women picking carefully along the beach to avoid ruining their slippers. "Save for the white glare of the breakers, the sea was a great wind-crossed void. From the throng of charming women floated the perfume of many flowers. Later there floated to them a body with a calm face of an Irish type." [14] As "Flanagan" concludes, the shipwreck has been diminished to the mere disruption of a dance.

"The Open Boat" is a story of the effect of a shipwreck on the consciousness of a survivor; "Flanagan" is first an adventure story of a tugboat captain and his filibustering expedition. It becomes, at

12 Ibid.
13 Ibid.
14 Ibid., 108.

its conclusion, a comment on the indifference of the partygoers, who, reveling in their own dream world, resent the intrusion of unpleasant events from the outside world. Although the dance is ruined, the revelers finally see not a person, but only a body, a type, washed up on shore. The reader is left with the impression that, for the hotel guests, the wreck is only a minor interruption. The next evening things will be back to normal in the escapist, self-centered life of the resort.

When Crane went to Cuba in 1898, he drew upon his experiences there and in Tampa to write another story with, at least in part, a Florida setting. "The Clan of No-Name" has been called by one critic, "Perhaps the most artistically complex and thematically sophisticated of Crane's stories of war." Crane himself called this story a peach. "I love it devotedly," he said. "I *love* this story."[15] "The Clan of No-Name" is at the same time a love story and a war story. The dual plot is paralleled by the frame structure of the story in which both the opening and closing scenes take place in a secluded garden in Tampa. Juxtaposed between these scenes is the tale of the death of young Manolo who is fighting with the Americans in Cuba. While his beloved Margharita thinks of him in her garden at home, Manolo dies a grisly death by a machete in a trench.

Just as in "Flanagan" Crane contrasts the grim reality of the shipwreck with the gaiety of the dance, so in "The Clan of No-Name" is the idyllic setting, the garden with a plashing fountain in which Margharita waits for Manolo, contrasted with the fetid, ugly ditch in which Manolo dies. In "Clan" Margharita crassly and casually betrays her love for Manolo. At the same time that he is fighting, a photograph of her in his pocket, Margharita is receiving calls from a Mr. Smith, a wealthy Tampa businessman. In the opening scene, before Manolo's death, Margharita half-heartedly refuses Smith's overtures. In the closing scene Margharita leaves the garden and goes into the stuffy little parlor to receive her suitor, where she coyly accepts his proposal of marriage.

15 James Nagel, "Stephen Crane's 'The Clan of No-Name,'" *Kyusha American Literature*, XIV (1972), 34; Fredson Bowers (ed.), *Tales of War* (Charlottesville, 1971), cxii. Vol. VI of Bowers (ed.), *The Works of Stephen Crane*, 10 vols.

Margharita's shallowness, evidenced by the speed with which she betrays Manolo's memory after his death, is heightened by her beauty and by her lovely surroundings. Like the revelers at the beach, she does not want her dream world disturbed. She burns Manolo's picture, and, encouraged by her greedy mother, looks forward to a life of ease as the new Mrs. Smith.

Crane's use of Florida in his fiction is complex. Certainly the most skillful use of setting is in "The Open Boat," in which setting becomes an instrument of inward growth. In "Flanagan" and "The Clan of No-Name" Florida is used as a frivolous counterpoint to the harshness of the outside world, be it sea or battleground. In these stories the escapist lure of the hotel courtyard or the private garden, both pictured with plashing fountains, is strong. In these dreamlike settings the real world seems far away indeed.

In his own life Crane was never free from the cares of everyday life. The bill collectors dunned him even in the last months of his life at Brede Manor where he was writing steadily in the futile hope of surmounting his debts. The idyllic world of Brede Manor ultimately failed him just as the Hotel de Dreme had failed him in Florida, and in his Florida fiction Crane paints a portrait both sympathetic to and satiric of an idyllic setting and its Eden-seeking inhabitants.

Among the many friends, including Joseph Conrad and Harold Frederic, that Crane had during his brief period in England was a writer, much older than Crane, who would soon return to the United States and would experience in Florida some of what Stephen Crane had seen. Henry James was returning to America after twenty years abroad. The author of more than twenty published books was, at the age of sixty-one, coming home again. What James found in 1904 when he returned to America surprised and in many ways disillusioned him. American civilization had grown bigger but not better. As one critic has noted, James felt "America had urbanized itself without acquiring urbanity."[16]

---

16 Alan Trachtenberg, "The American Scene: Versions of the City," *Massachusetts Review*, VIII (Spring, 1967), 283.

The Florida portion of James's tour made a great impression upon him. He responded strongly to the subtropical climate and the luxuriant natural settings. The soft breezes and ocean expanses were all pleasing to him. In many ways Florida fulfilled his expectations of a paradisic land, and his indictments of Florida were directed not at the place itself but at the hordes of what he termed the "boarders," those denizens of hotel life whose presence threatened to overpower Florida's delicate charms. The same pushy, crowding Americans whose activities had, in James's opinion, spoiled most of the rest of the country, were now ravaging Florida as well.

James began his American tour in August, 1904. After a day in New York, he set off for New England, where after a visit of several weeks at his brother William's summer place at Chocorua, New Hampshire, he visited Boston, Cambridge, and Salem. He returned then to New York, visited Newport, and then in the winter of 1904–1905 started South to avoid the northern cold. James's impressions of New England, the eastern seaboard, and the South make up *The American Scene*, first published in 1907. He intended to write a second volume recounting his experiences during the lecture tour he made in the spring of 1905 when he went west to Indianapolis, Chicago, St. Louis, and finally to California. But James was weary after his protracted journey. When he returned to England in the summer of 1905 he began writing his account of his ten-month journey. After completing in *The American Scene* the account of his journey through his visit to the South, he decided not to write of his western experience.

As Leon Edel has noted, *The American Scene* for the most part "has been neglected and certainly misread." An example of this misreading is found in a contemporary review. "Mr. Henry James has spent a holiday in America, and like other scribblers, better and worse, would fain recover his travelling expenses by printing his impressions. Only that—and nothing more!"[17] Although this review

17 Leon Edel, "Speaking of Books: Henry James Looked Ahead," *New York Times Book Review* (November 12, 1967), 2; [Y. Y.], Review of Henry James's *The American Scene* in *Bookman*, XXXI (March, 1907), 265.

unfairly denigrates James's purpose in *The American Scene*, it reflects the problems later critics have had with the book. One does not expect a travel book from Henry James; since *The American Scene* is neither a novel nor a treatise on the art of fiction, what does one do with it? The answer generally has been to relegate the work to a minor place in James's canon.

Those critics who have recognized the importance of *The American Scene*, however, have emphasized the strengths of the work. In a sympathetic treatment, W. H. Auden pointed up the enormous task James had undertaken.

> Of all possible subjects, travel is the most difficult for an artist, as it is the easiest for a journalist. For the latter, the interesting ever is the new, the extraordinary, the comic, the shocking, and all that the peripatetic journalist requires is a flair for being on the spot where and when such events happen—the rest is merely passive typewriter thumping; meaning, relation, importance, are not his quarry. The artist, on the other hand, is deprived of his most treasured liberty, the freedom to invent; successfully to extract importance from historical personal events without ever departing from them, free only to select and never to modify or to add, calls for imagination of a very high order.[18]

Auden probably overstates his position, but his comments amplify why Edward King failed to create a truly artistic portrait of Florida where Stephen Crane managed to succeed. James was limited by the necessity of a rigid attention to detail, but in *The American Scene* he achieves an artful portrayal of the effect of the American scene upon one's consciousness.

James's purpose, then, was not merely to write a travelogue. Frederick Hoffman calls *The American Scene* "the most important of all assessments of the American self." Peter Buitenhuis concurs. "With the exception of Tocqueville's *Democracy in America*, it is hard to think of a more subtle and penetrating study of American life."[19]

---

18 W. H. Auden, "Henry James's 'The American Scene,'" *Horizon*, XV (1947), 77.

19 Frederick J. Hoffman, "Freedom and Conscious Form: Henry James and the American Self," *Virginia Quarterly Review*, XXXVII (1961), 277; Peter

James possessed the unique vision of an American, who by having been away for twenty years could view his native land with a fresh perspective. That perspective was especially fresh when James began his journey South, for though he had known New York and New England before, the South was unexplored territory to him. As Edel notes, to the young James the South had been the Confederacy.[20] At the turn of the century, though he looked for and found traces of a romantic past in Richmond and Charleston, it was a defeated Old South now becoming a more commercialized New South that he found.

When Crane visited Florida, the railroad line ended in Jacksonville. Only a few years later, by the time of James's visit, the railroad extended down the Florida east coast to Palm Beach, and the Gold Coast was flowering into its prime. Tourists and settlers were flooding to south Florida, so that in effect, modern Florida tourism was underway. Henry James witnessed this phenomenon and, for the most part, was appalled by it. Florida was becoming another Newport; in this case, though, it was the winter season that drew the rich and fashionable. No longer the haven for invalids that Sidney Lanier had observed, Florida, and especially its lower east coast, was becoming a playground for the rich.

James's visit to Florida lasted less than six days, and it was filled with both disappointments and pleasant surprises. He had left Charleston on a Sunday morning in a disgruntled state when a porter had set in the mud a travel bag that he was shortly required to carry on his knees. After a stop in Savannah at noon, the train arrived in Jacksonville that night. The following morning he went on to Palm Beach for a visit of several days. After Palm Beach his last major stop was St. Augustine, before his return journey north.

James had found much to disappoint him in his American tour before arriving in Florida. New York had changed from a provincial

---

Buitenhuis, *The Grasping Imagination: The American Writings of Henry James* (Toronto, 1970), 182.

20 Leon Edel, Introduction to James, *The American Scene*, x.

trade center to a crassly commercial metropolis. Ugly skyscrapers obliterated the landscape. Above all, James could find in his native land no sense of tradition. No place or building seemed sacred. Anything could be torn down to make way for something bigger, which must assuredly be better.

In the context of his general sense of disappointment, James's Florida experience is somewhat unique. In Florida he was also disappointed, but he was charmed as well. His reactions were complex. He saw in Florida the best and the worst of America. In its balmy weather, surrounded by tropical foliage, James felt entranced. At the same time he was finally repulsed by the hoards of pleasure-seekers who flocked to Palm Beach—lured by the very beauty that so enchanted James.

James's love-hate relationship with Florida is reflected in each of the Florida settings he treats—Jacksonville, Palm Beach, and St. Augustine. In each he sensed something to charm him and something to disappoint him as well. His first night in Florida he sat in the public garden adjoining his hotel in Jacksonville and found that the Florida evening was everything he had hoped for. "The air was divinely soft—it was such a Southern night as I had dreamed of." There follows a curious passage in which James is both attracted and repelled by the garden. "I had come out to smoke for the evening's end, and it mattered not a scrap that the public garden was new and scant and crude, and that Jacksonville is not a name to conjure with; I still could sit there quite in the spirit, for the hour, of Byron's immortal question as to the verity of his Italian whereabouts: *was* this the Mincio, *were* those the distant turrets of Verona. . . . I projected myself, for the time, after Byron's manner, into the exquisite sense of the dream come true" (*AS*, 432–33).

James was enchanted by the St. Johns River—"Byronically foolish," he called it. "The river," he said, "served for my Mincio—which it moreover so greatly surpassed in extent and beauty." As he sat he began to list his impressions of his surroundings. "For that was the charm—that so preposterously, with the essential notes of the impression so happily struck, the velvet air, the extravagant plants, the palms, the oranges, the cacti, the architectural fountain, the florid local monument, the cheap and easy exoticism, the sense as of people feeding, off in the background, very much *al fresco*, that is on queer things and with flaring lights—one might almost have been in a corner of Naples or of Genoa" (*AS*, 433-34).

Anticipating the rest of his visit in Florida, James found, "The note of Florida emerged for me then on the vulgar little dusky—and dusty—Jacksonville *piazzetta*." And what would the note be; in writing *The American Scene* James looked forward and back; in Jacksonville he had "virtually foretasted" all his visit would be. "Florida was quite remorselessly to appear to me a complex of few interweavings" (*AS*, 434-35).

The major part of James's Florida visit was spent in Palm Beach, and it was there that he saw what were, for him, both the best and worst aspects of Florida. His initial impression was marred by the fact that, the train arriving late, an extremely hungry James was denied an evening meal at the hotel. He did not fail to remark on what he considered an American characteristic—a sumptuous, expensive hotel that failed to provide every amenity for its guests. This would never happen in Europe, but Americans simply did not know any better.

As in Jacksonville, James relished his surroundings.

> The velvet air, the colour of the sea, the "royal" palms, clustered here and there, and, in their nobleness of beauty, their single sublime distinction, putting every other mark and sign to the blush, these are the principal figures of the sum—these, with the custom of the short dip into the jungle, at two or three points of which, approached by charming, winding wood-ways, the small but genial fruit-farm offers hospitality—offers it in all the succulence of the admirable pale-skinned orange and the huge sunwarmed grapefruit, plucked from the low bough, where it fairly bumps your cheek for solicitation, and partaken of, on the spot, as the immortal ladies of Cranford partook of dessert (*AS*, 449).

On one hand, Palm Beach might be seen, with its beach and lake and pleasant groves, as a veritable Eden. The hotels, the Breakers and the Royal Poinciana, might first appear as heavenly mansions. But James imposes on this idyllic picture an overlay of pushing crowds. The boarders, as he calls them, are the main attraction at Palm Beach. One comes to Palm Beach, we learn, not so much to bask in the idyllic setting as to observe who else is there. James notes, "There, as nowhere else, in America, one would find Vanity Fair in full blast—and Vanity Fair not scattered, not discriminated and parcelled out, as among the comparative privacies and ancientries of Newport, but compressed under one vast cover, enclosed in a single huge *vitrine*" (*AS*, 449).

Again and again James contrasted these elements of lovely nature and the pushing crowds. Of subtropical Florida he said, "The softness was divine—like something mixed, in a huge silver crucible, as an elixir, and then liquidly scattered" (*AS*, 451). Always nearby, however, was "the other show," the spectacle of Vanity Fair.

In "Daisy Miller" James considered at length the condition of the American girl. Palm Beach was to provide him with examples far more spectacular, representing to James the epitome of the effects of American society. In his concluding remarks on Palm Beach he raised an intriguing question. "As for the younger persons, of whom there were many, as for the young girls in especial, they were as perfectly in their element as goldfish in a crystal jar: a form of exhibition suggesting but one question or mystery. Was it they who had invented it, or had it inscrutably invented *them*?" (*AS*, 456). The question about the young girls could be applied to the larger spectacle as well. What were these people, this American society, really doing in Palm Beach? As James has noted, in the midst of some of the most spectacular scenery in the world, the real show was the boarders—the artificial resort life was, for these people, the real scene. Were these real people, one wondered, or was Vanity Fair just a vast play being performed? Amused as he was by the spectacle, James did not hesitate to point out the emptiness of it. A few decades later Ring Lardner would write a story of a man who went on a Florida vacation without ever seeing the sun and the beaches and the palms—he would be totally immersed in the social life of the hotel.

The last part of the Florida section in *The American Scene* treats St. Augustine. Comparing Palm Beach and St. Augustine, James noted that if the social scene at Palm Beach was a disappointment, the much-touted historic aspects of St. Augustine also left much to be desired. He had been prepared by magazine articles with their charming illustrations to find a quaint little town steeped in history. He found instead a poverty of relics, and hinted that the citizens were busily engaged in producing more.

In typical Jamesian fashion he concluded that St. Augustine proved to be "primarily, and of course quite legitimately, but an hotel, of the first magnitude—an hotel indeed so remarkable and so pleasant that I wondered what call there need ever have been upon it to prove anything else." The Ponce de Leon, modeled on a Moorish castle with turrets and cloisters, arcades and fountains came "as near producing, all by itself, the illusion of romance as a highly modern, a most cleverly-constructed and smoothly-administered great modern caravansery can come" (*AS*, 459).

One other thing in St. Augustine pleased James—the old Spanish fort, "the empty, sunny, grassy shell by the low, pale shore; the mild, time-silvered quadrilateral that, under the care of a single exhibitory veteran and with the still milder remnant of a town-gate near it, preserves alone, to any effect of appreciable emphasis, the memory of the Spanish occupation" (*AS*, 459–60).

James's disappointment could have been predicted. How could one who adored the fixed structure of society and the deep sense of the past in Europe have been anything but disappointed by raw, new hotels set in land recently reclaimed from the jungle and peopled by the rich, many of whom laid claim to their social standing not on the basis of blood but on the size of their recently acquired bank accounts? And even if it could call itself the oldest city in America, how could little St. Augustine compare favorably with the European capitals of the world that James knew and loved?

Critics have noted the harsh treatment James gave to Florida in *The American Scene*. On the contrary, however, given James's predispositions, it seems remarkable that he was seduced by Florida to the extent that he was. Every compliment was qualified with a little sniping, but James's concluding paragraph on Florida was surprisingly sympathetic.

> There was no doubt, under the influence of this last look, that Florida still had, in her ingenuous, not at all insidious way, the secret of pleasing, and that even round about me the vagueness was still an appeal. The vagueness was warm, the vagueness was bright, the vagueness was sweet, being scented and flowered and fruited; above all, the vagueness was somehow consciously and confessedly weak. I made out in it something of the look of the charming shy face that desires to communicate and that yet has just too little expression. What it would fain say was that it really knew itself unequal to any extravagance of demand upon it, but that (if it might so plead to one's tenderness) it would always do its gentle best. I found the plea, for myself, I may declare, exquisite and irresistible: the Florida of that particular tone was a Florida adorable (*AS*, 460).

The 1907 American edition of *The American Scene* ended with James's musings on Florida—a mixed impression perhaps, but not condemning. What Harper and Brothers omitted in the edition was contained in the English edition of the work, a five-page account of James's conclusions as he sat on the train returning North.

Reflecting on his travels thus far, James plunged into a nightmare reverie of what he had seen and experienced.[21] He had come back from Europe to discover the spirit of American life. After months of travel, he could address his country this way: "it wouldn't be to *you* I should be looking in any degree for beauty or for charm. Beauty and charm would be for me in the solitude you have ravaged, and I should owe you my grudge for every disfigurement and every violence, for every wound with which you have caused the face of the land to bleed" (*AS*, 463).

James could not forgive his countrymen for the ugliness they had inflicted on the vast continent. "You touch the great lonely land—as

---

21 Edel, "Speaking of Books," 72.

one feels it still to be—only to plant upon it some ugliness about which, never dreaming of the grace of apology or contrition, you then proceed to brag with a cynicism all your own" (*AS*, 463). The raw newness of the ugly buildings, the total American ignorance of tradition and a sense of the past were an affront to James that he could not forgive. The ultimate heresy was that, from Newport to Palm Beach, every manifestation of American society was, at its basis, vulgar.

What James saw in Florida was perhaps the culmination of all that he had come to despair of during his tour of America. Everywhere Americans were creating blights upon the environment, and everywhere the almighty dollar was creating a new social strata that was pushy, brassy, and ignorant of even the most basic social forms. Seeing this Vanity Fair in Palm Beach—among the beauty of the flowers, in the soft balmy air—seeing a thronging mass so intent upon its empty pleasures that it did not even notice the lovely surroundings, James realized all that he had sensed everywhere he went.

Yes, Florida was "thin." St. Augustine had but a slim history to offer; Emerson had called its relics "dim vestiges of a romantic past," but for the vulgar rich in the vulgar hotels, it was but pearls before swine anyway. Florida itself might ultimately disappoint, but what had been done to Florida—the wounds inflicted upon it—was the ultimate disappointment.

The experiences of Crane and James in Florida were very different. It was a stroke of fortune, a freak accident, that Florida provided the basis for some of Crane's best fiction. In his work also can be seen the progression from simple reporting (as evidenced in his newspaper account of the *Commodore* wreck) to a transmutation of raw material into art. Florida had inspired earlier writers, but with Crane the raw material had at last been treated by an imagination of the highest order.

Henry James's experience—more ordered, more compressed in time, subject to no accident other than a missed meal—is of a different quality and degree than Crane's. Unlike Crane, James did not cast Florida as a basis for his fiction. But it is equally true that

James's treatment of Florida was also more than mere reporting. The Florida section of *The American Scene* is an account of what happened to James, where he stayed, what he saw. But more than that, it is, as it was for Crane, a representation of the effect of the surroundings on the consciousness of the observer. *The American Scene* is more than a report of James's trip; it is an intense account of what this journey meant to him, what impressions it was to make upon his evaluation of America. The interior landscape, then, the effect of Florida on James's thought, is finally more important than the exterior scene. In *The American Scene* Florida was to become, more than it had ever been before, a realized metaphor. No longer simply pictured as an idyllic or faraway land, Florida for James was a vision of all that was potentially good and beautiful in America and all that was ultimately wrong.

The bank of the St. Johns River in the late 1880s

The *Osceola* steams up the Oklawaha River, *ca.* 1886.

Silver Springs, *ca.* 1886

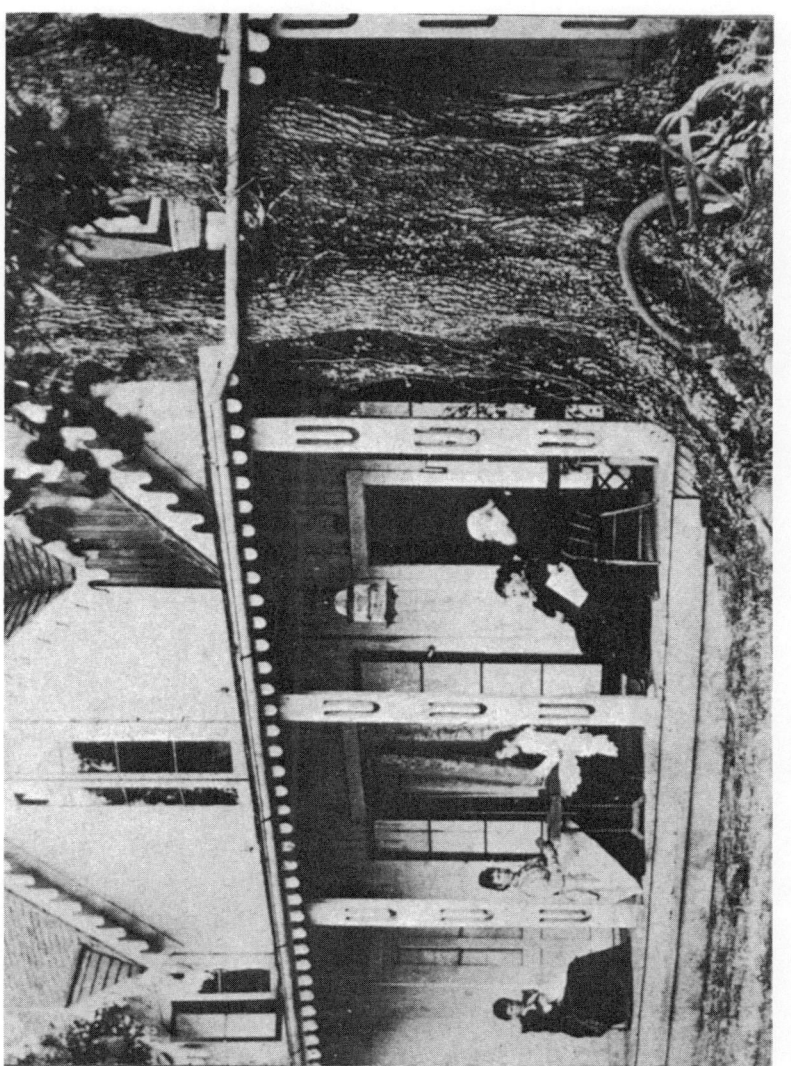

The Stowe family on the porch of their house in Mandarin

Spanish-American War soldiers being served dinner in their camp near Tampa

Fort San Marcos, near St. Augustine, in the mid-1880s. Henry James visited the fort two decades later.

The Breakers, Palm Beach

The Ponce de Leon Hotel, St. Augustine, 1905

Tea on the lawn at the Belleview Biltmore Hotel, Belleair, 1920s

A tea dance at the coconut grove of the Royal Poinciana Hotel, Palm Beach

Marjorie Kinnan Rawlings' home at Cross Creek

Ernest Hemingway's home in Key West

IV
The Garden Spot of God's Green Footstool

> They was about two dozen uniformed Ephs on the job to meet us. And when I seen 'em all grab for our baggage with one hand and hold the other out, face up, I knowed why they called it Palm Beach.
>
> —Ring Lardner
> "Gullible's Travels"

First as a young sports reporter who was making a name for himself in the 1910s and 1920s, and later as one of America's best-known columnists who made frequent vacations to Florida with his wife, Ring Lardner was witness to the boom-and-bust era of Florida's history. "It would hardly be possible," wrote a Ring Lardner critic, "to conceive of a greater contrast than exists between Lardner's fictional world and that of Hawthorne or James."[1] But James's Palm Beach sketches and Lardner's accounts of the American booboisie in Florida bear some

---

1 Walton R. Patrick, *Ring Lardner* (New York, 1963), 150.

striking resemblances. James wrote of the pushing hordes who were drawn to Florida. A decade or so later Ring Lardner portrayed Florida as a magnet to the rest of the country, offering a variety of seductive promises, an escapist place of resorts for those who wanted to "get away from it all," but who actually entered the same frenetic sort of life in Palm Beach and Miami, and a place of retirement havens for "golden agers" who found that the fountain of youth would elude them in Florida as well. Sometimes cynical, sometimes tender, Lardner's stories and sketches were of a Florida that, lovely in and of itself, could not always meet the expectations of those who went there, and a Florida that was being overpowered by the money-grubbing ethos of American society.

In the ten years or so that passed between James's brief Florida visit of 1905 and Lardner's first of many visits there, remarkable changes were taking place in the state that would reflect both its escapist appeal to the American people and its concurrent incorporation into the mainstream of American economic and social life. With the election in 1904 of Napoleon B. Broward as Florida's governor, the state began to implement Broward's proposals for reclaiming Everglades lands through draining; such plans had been proposed in the late nineteenth century but never before carried out to such a great extent. Although there would be problems with flooding, and the initial boom of sales of 1910 would taper off, the Everglades development was a portent of future land development that would take place in the 1920s when John S. Collins and other northern investors would finance the development of what would become the Miami Gold Coast.

The early decades of the twentieth century brought with them the influx of automobiles into Florida. In the administration of Governor Park Trammell (1913–1917) taxes were levied to establish a better system of roads in the state. Not only did the improvement of roads promote tourism, it also created access for a special kind of visitor—the tin-can tourist. Thousands came annually to Florida and stayed in tourist camps.

For those who did not want to brave the tin-can camps but wished to avoid the high costs of the expensive resorts of Palm Beach and Miami, another option was the smaller tourist courts and rooms available. In addition to providing accommodations for the seasonal traveler, a number of places in Florida were attracting older people, retirees from harsher climates of the North and Midwest. Especially on Florida's west coast, at such places as St. Petersburg, a growing number of older people came south to warm themselves in the sun and engage in such moderate entertainments as horseshoes, cards, and roque.

The most dramatic series of events in Florida in the early twentieth century was the boom-and-bust period of the 1920s. As Dovell notes, "An unexpected result of the first world war on Florida came with the influx of winter visitors who were unable to pursue their pleasures on the European rivieras and so traveled to the Florida resorts on the east and west coasts of the peninsula."[2] This flooding of visitors into Florida together with Collins' development of Miami Beach and the development by George E. Merrick of Coral Gables precipitated the Florida land boom which peaked in 1925.

The frantic speculation in land that included both honest businessmen and swindlers alike has been noted as "but an expression of the . . . business optimism throughout the United States which had been generated by the first world war." By 1925 Florida's population was almost three times what it had been at the beginning of the century. In the early 1920s Florida was up for grabs for land buyers and developers, but in Florida's case at least, not even paradise was immune from hard times. A series of events took place that created a temporary setback to the state's development. In rapid succession Florida suffered from two devastating hurricanes, the West Indian hurricane of September, 1926, which created havoc on the east coast, and another hurricane in 1928 in which as many as two thousand people were drowned in settlements near Lake Okeechobee. The stock market crash of 1929 and subsequent bank failures brought the death knell for the twenties boom period. Although Flor-

2 Dovell, *Florida*, II, 769.

ida would be buoyed by continuing tourism and investments in the 1930s and would suffer less from the depression than many other places, the frenetic, fast-paced, high-living period of the 1920s was gone forever.[3]

In many ways Ring Lardner was the ideal satirist to create a portrait of Florida in the 1920s, for his own life was emblematic of the fast-changing way of living that characterized America at the time. In Florida he saw the embodiment of the boom and bust of the American dream. Lardner's boyhood and youth had been spent in Niles, Michigan, where he had been born in 1885. In November, 1907, he left Niles permanently. Although he would return for visits, it would never be home again. The break with Niles, as one of Lardner's biographers has noted, was a taking leave of an insular, well-ordered life. Jonathan Yardley has fancifully portrayed Lardner's hometown and what it stood for. "More than Niles was coming to a close for Ring. A way of life was ending, the gentler life of turn-of-the-century upper-class America. It was a life shaded by parasols, a life lived to the peaceful pace of a paddle-wheel steamer idly inching its way across a lake, a life frozen brightly on a wall by the lamp of a magic lantern."[4] Lardner had left Niles, but in a decade or so he would find that all that Niles had represented would escape him as well; in a few years the Victorian and Edwardian world of his childhood, so comfortable to Henry James as well, would be destroyed.

Having disappointed his parents in failing to obtain a college degree, Lardner was determined to make a success in the newspaper world. His life after 1907 was in many ways characteristic of the new faster-paced American life that would culminate in the feverish pitch of the 1920s. His early newspaper years in Chicago and New York were lived at a murderous pace, especially after Lardner married his sweetheart, Ellis Abbott, also the product of an upper-class family and a graduate of a prestigious woman's school. Driven by his desire to maintain a lifestyle appropriate to Ellis' background

---

[3] Ibid., 771, 776, 782–83.
[4] Jonathan Yardley, *Ring: A Biography of Ring Lardner* (New York, 1977), 71.

and upbringing, Lardner formed in his early years a relentless pattern of work that he would maintain throughout his life.

Lardner's own life can be seen as a metaphor for the American lifestyle he would analyze and parody. First, he had made the break with small-time, middle America and moved to the city, as so many others would do in the early decades of the twentieth century. As a sports writer, the role for which many readers remember him, Lardner epitomized the American love for baseball, the all-American sport. During those early years as a reporter, Lardner traveled extensively, following the major teams. This nomadic life-style was to characterize the remainder of his life; it was also to reflect the rootlessness that would be a major facet of American life after the First World War.

The parallels between Lardner's ultimate disillusionment with baseball (though he continued to write about it throughout his life) and the general loss of innocence in America after 1914 has not gone unnoticed by critics. The Black Sox scandal, in which seven members of the White Sox team threw the World Series for $100,000, had a profound effect upon him. "Baseball, on which his whole career and reputation had been founded, had lost its enchantment. And so had a great many other things. It was not in baseball alone that the old rules were being changed and the old standards crumbling away."[5] When Lardner left Niles as a young man, he had not abandoned the old principles of honor, stability, tradition. The Black Sox scandal showed that heroes could have feet of clay, that anyone could sell out to the almighty dollar. And cheating in baseball was only emblematic of a new code that began to characterize the American way of life—the get-rich-quick schemes, the shearing away of roots, and, indeed, the national loss of innocence at the end of the war. If Lardner had stayed in Niles he might not have felt these changes so sharply, but his own way of life not only underscored the changes in the American lifestyle; his traveling brought

---

5 Donald Elder, *Ring Lardner* (Garden City, N.Y., 1956), 163. See also Yardley, *Ring*, 213.

him to the very places that epitomized so much of what Lardner saw wrong with America.

In his early career as a baseball reporter he had traveled continually, to such places as Florida and California. After his marriage to Ellis, even when they had established a permanent home on Long Island, they made annual winter vacations—usually to Florida, often accompanied by their close friends, the Grantland Rices. One of Lardner's favorite spots was Belleair near St. Petersburg. Here he and Grantland Rice would play golf, and Lardner would observe the foibles of the vacationers.

Elizabeth Evans, in her study of Lardner, has commented on his chief subject matter, the bourgeoisie of the 1920s. "Symptomatic of the breaking up of American life in the twenties, they are transient, always on trains, in hotels, at race tracks. Only skirting the society they cannot join, they are incapable of real pleasure."[6] Lardner was perhaps in a class above his characters, but he could masterfully create a language through which to express their thoughts and feelings. His syndicated newspaper columns were often written from the point of view of the Boob, and the narrative technique of his stories proceeds in the same way. As Walton Patrick has observed, "The hallmark of the typical Lardner character is that he is unconscious that his words show him in a light entirely different from the one intended or that they convey an idea the opposite of the one he thinks he is expressing." Lardner's method in his stories was to reveal the subjective qualities of his characters only through external description. He never enters their minds; instead, as Patrick notes: "Insofar as he reveals the subjective qualities of his characters at all, he reveals them indirectly through what they say about themselves and others. The peculiar force of Lardner's narrative method is that he makes the reader see and hear and hence form his own judgment of the characters from their external rather than from their internal qualities."[7]

6 Elizabeth Evans, *Ring Lardner* (New York, 1979), 128.
7 Patrick, *Ring Lardner*, 117, 118.

Lardner made many references to Florida in his writing. A number of his columns were datelined from there, and in those newspaper accounts he often spoofed the social customs of the tourist. There are also numerous passing references to Florida in his fiction, usually in the context of a discussion by the characters of where to go on vacation. Lardner also made an unsuccessful venture into writing a movie script, entitled *The New Klondike*, which pictured Florida as the site of the second gold rush, only this time the gold was real estate. Before the bubble burst at the onset of the depression, Florida real estate was considered an excellent investment. Lardner, however, never speculated in it and was spared the terrible ill effects to the Florida economy of the great hurricane of 1928 and the real estate bust that followed.

Lardner's best and most complex use of Florida in his work appears in three of his short stories, two of which—"Gullible's Travels" and "The Golden Honeymoon"—are among his best-known work. "Sun Cured," a lesser-known story, is a scathing portrait of one type of Florida vacationer and a satiric picture of Miami resort life.

"Gullible's Travels," the title story for Lardner's short story collection published in 1917, grew out of his vacation experience in Palm Beach the previous year. When Henry James visited there in 1905, Palm Beach was new, and though already a crowded, pushy place, it was essentially a resort for the extremely rich. Ten years later, when Lardner arrived, the resort had grown even more. Still a playground for the idle rich, it had also become a place where those who aspired to high society were drawn.

"Gullible's Travels" is the story of a middle-class couple with more money than taste who engage a room at the Royal Poinciana and make a two-week foray into the Palm Beach social scene, with disastrous results. The anonymous narrator of the story, known only as Mr. is, as Maxwell Geismar has noted, "a partial extension of the Busher [of Lardner's earlier baseball stories]. He is the 'Wise-Boob' from the sticks who is being taken for a ride by a social system whose primary aim was 'mobility upwards'—which was converting all these ignorant or innocent farm boys (and small-town souls) into a 'lower-middle class'; which was elevating this social stratum, in turn, to a 'middle class,' and then—by the simple instrumentality of instant cash in the Teens and Twenties—into a new American and social 'aristocracy.'"[8] Not only is the boob the same character Lardner's reader saw in the Busher stories, but the setting—Palm Beach instead of the baseball diamond—has become the stage for showing the rise and the corruption of middle America.

The Mr. of "Gullible's Travels," largely persuaded by his wife to make the trip, recounts the desperate attempts of the Mrs. to take part in the gilded world of Palm Beach. When they arrive at the station of the Royal Poinciana, the husband comments, "When I seen 'em all grab for our luggage with one hand and hold the other out, face up, I knowed why they called it Palm Beach" (*GT*, 66). They go through the daily rituals of ocean bathing, afternoon tea at Coconut Grove, evening dinner and dances, while the Mrs. tries to convince herself that they are fitting in.

As Geismar remarks, the Gullibles' "gilded 'vacations' are an inferno of social snobbery, boredom, and wasted money." The Florida trip, which was to be a dream-come-true for the Mrs., becomes instead a nightmare. "What really comes out, through all the elaborate, expensive southern vacation resorts in *Gullible's Travels* itself, is the high cost of torture. 'After supper we said good-bye to the night clerk and twenty-two bucks!'"[9]

Their boredom with the social activities, and the husband's constant suffering over the high prices he must pay are torture enough, but the final blow comes when the Mrs. is mistaken for a maid by a wealthy socialite who orders her to bring some towels. Finally crushed in her vain social aspirations, the Mrs. agrees it is time to go home.

Although the title of the story implies gullibility and the Mr. is easily seen as a boob, it would be an oversimplification to say that

---

8 Maxwell Geismar (ed.), *The Ring Lardner Reader* (New York, 1963), xviii.
9 *Ibid.*, xix–xx.

Lardner is simply parodying the narrator of the story. Donald Elder notes as much in his perceptive analysis of the narrator as "a sardonic and wise type who comments on the other characters and on the action. . . . He is an average American who speaks ungrammatically and spells as he pronounces, but he is no fool. If he is gullible, it is because he is indulgent and easygoing rather than stupid; and he pricks the pretenses of his wife and his friends with a sharp sarcasm. . . . he is sensible and practical; and he is continually showing up the brainlessness and fatuity of his fellows. He is a character with whom an unwary reader might identify himself."[10] The Mr. may be the boob, but he is also Ring Lardner poking fun at his surroundings. Even more important, through Gullible, Lardner is making a humorous yet grim comment on the inanities we put ourselves through for the upward mobility that would seem to lead nowhere. For if the reader laughs at the grammatical shortcomings and social ineptitudes of Mr. and Mrs. Gullible, he must also question the worth of the very things for which they are striving. Lardner's picture of Palm Beach is an even harsher indictment than was James's Vanity Fair portrayal. The vacation paradise becomes in Lardner's story nothing more than a gilded nightmare—an overpriced, torturous place peopled by those too vapid to even notice how silly it all is.

Although Lardner occasionally stayed in Palm Beach, he much preferred the quieter resorts of Florida's west coast. A vacation in Belleair near St. Petersburg in 1922 resulted in another Florida story, one that in its publication and critical reaction would create somewhat of a furor. "The Golden Honeymoon," which Lardner wrote at Belleair, was turned down by George Horace Lorimer at the *Post* who felt that the story, unlike any of Lardner's earlier work, would be ill received by his fans. Lardner then sent the story to Ray Long at *Cosmopolitan*. Not only was Long happy to publish a Lardner story, he sensed that this one was exceptionally fine. "I see what the *Post* meant," he wrote Lardner. "That story isn't the usual Ring Lardner

---

10 Elder, *Ring Lardner*, 135.

story. All it is is a fine piece of sympathetic human interest writing. . . . I shall be very proud to publish it."[11]

In "The Golden Honeymoon" Lardner was treating another, newer facet of Florida: the budding retirement communities and tourist resorts, built not as playgrounds for the rich but as meccas for the elderly. If Florida could not quite guarantee a fountain of youth, it did offer a mecca for rejuvenation, a place where "senior citizens" (the term would soon be invented) could warm their bones in the sun and while away the afternoons in such nonstrenuous games as horseshoes.

"The Golden Honeymoon" is the story of a New Jersey couple who spend a winter month in St. Petersburg celebrating fifty years of marriage. As in "Gullible's Travels," the narrator is an older man. Lardner makes his narrator interminably mundane as the story opens and closes with tedious accounts of the train's timetables; every stop and its hour are noted by the narrator. Equally tedious are his character descriptions; the people on the train are described in terms of a few variables: hometown, occupation, Rotary affiliation, and so on. In the narrator's descriptions Lardner allows a little joke on himself when the narrator describes nearby Belleair as "the winter headquarters for the golf dudes and everybody that got off there had their bag of sticks, as many as ten and twelve in a bag. Women and all. When I was a young man we called it shinny and only needed one club to play with and about one game of it would of been a-plenty for some of these dudes, the way we played it" (GH, 119–20).

Arriving in St. Petersburg the narrator and his wife, called Mother in the story, soon establish themselves into the typical routine of "the Poor Man's Palm Beach." They find a decent, clean cafeteria in which they take almost all their meals, visit the city park daily where card games, checkers, roque and horseshoes are played, and take in a movie almost every night. Into this quiet little setting, Lardner soon introduces all the elements for a domestic drama

---

11 Yardley, *Ring*, 249–50.

when Mother encounters the wife of the beau she had rejected some fifty years ago. The Hartsells become their constant companions, and now the narrator must suffer nightly card games at which he and Mrs. Hartsell always lose to Mother and Mr. Hartsell.

Like two knights jousting for their ladies, the narrator and Mr. Hartsell are each driven to show his superiority. The narrator seethes because, saddled with the inept Mrs. Hartsell as a partner, he loses in the nightly card games. He has a temporary triumph when he trounces Mr. Hartsell at checkers in the park, but his victory is short-lived when Hartsell, who was "the luckiest pitcher I ever seen," beats him at horseshoes, leaving him humiliated and with a bleeding thumb.

The friendship with the Hartsells is strained when Mrs. Hartsell loses her teeth on the roque court while playing with Mother; it is brought to an end when, after losing still another game of cards, the narrator simply cannot endure Hartsell's comment "that he wouldn't never lose a game of cards if he could always have Mother for a partner." He replies, "Well, you had a chance fifty years ago to always have her for a partner, but you wasn't man enough to keep her" (*GH*, 138). Mother punishes her husband for his rudeness by not speaking to him for two days, but at length she reminds him that it is their golden honeymoon. They make their peace and salvage the remaining two days of their vacation.

Destined to become one of Lardner's best-known stories, "The Golden Honeymoon" aroused a storm of criticism. In a scathing review entitled "The Triangle of Hate," Clifton Fadiman called it "one of the most smashing indictments of a 'happy marriage' ever written, composed with a fury so gelid as to hide completely the bitter passion seething beneath every line. Under the level of homey sentiment lies a terrific contempt for this quarrelsome, vain, literal old couple, who for fifty years have disliked life and each other without ever having had the courage or the imagination to face the reality of their own meanness."[12]

12 *Ibid.*, 250–51.

The characters in "The Golden Honeymoon" may be mundane, the couple may quibble over trivia, but it is not a husband who hates his wife who can say: "I was just tired and all wrought up. I thank God you chose me instead of him as they's no other woman who I could of lived with all these years" (*GH*, 140). This may not be the stuff of romance, but there is certainly more of affection than of hate in his remarks. In his biography of Lardner, Yardley accurately observes that Lardner "understood, doubtless from watching the old folks of St. Pete from his perch at nearby Belleair, the unwritten rules that permitted these people to have their minor spats and running arguments while maintaining a foundation of affection and mutual understanding." Yardley finds in the story a good deal of "respect for two people who have managed to muddle through a half-century together."[13]

Equally extreme, though in a different direction, was H. L. Mencken's review of the story. "There is more of sheer reality in such a story as 'The Golden Honeymoon' than in the whole canon of Henry James, and there is also, I believe, more expert craftsmanship." As Yardley notes, "Mencken embraced Ring as an ally who in his fiction took the same view as Mencken in his journalism of the 'Low Down American.'"[14]

In his picture of middle-America-come-to-Florida, Lardner was again showing the foibles of the vacationers. Just as the Gullibles had subjected themselves to a torturous routine, the narrator and Mother enter a dull routine in St. Petersburg—here, though, the meals were two dollars instead of twenty-two.

Clearly, Lardner is poking fun at the narrator and Mother and at St. Petersburg and the old people who flock there, but in "The Golden Honeymoon" the satire is softened with affection. St. Petersburg is not, ultimately, the heavenly escape the honeymooners thought it might be, but Lardner's picture is a gentler one than his description of Palm Beach. "The Golden Honeymoon," perhaps

13 *Ibid.*, 251.
14 *Ibid.*, 286–87.

Lardner's best writing about Florida, is a portrait of old people. In this sketch of Florida's west coast Lardner shows the negation of Ponce de León's fountain of youth or the vain search for it. But if the quest for a renewed youth and vigor is unfulfilled, the couple in this story do realize what each has meant to the other.

A much less sympathetic account is Lardner's lesser-known story, "Sun Cured," which is contained in *Round-Up*, published in 1929. In this story two men meet on a train going to Florida and then encounter each other again four weeks later on a northbound train. In what is essentially a monologue (the insurance man, Ernie Fretts, seldom gives the other man, Walters, a chance to speak) we learn all the details of Fretts's Miami vacation. He tells Walters that he has been driving himself too hard in New York and that his office "girl" (a woman in her fifties) has insisted that her boss take a Florida vacation to restore his health.

Fretts is excited about his first trip to Florida. "I need just this kind of a trip—go down there where I don't know nobody and no girls pestering me all the w'ile, and be outdoors all day and exercise and breathe God's fresh air" (SC, 440). On the return trip, Fretts waxes enthusiastically over his wonderful trip. "No place like it in the world! . . . Say, I could write a book! I wished I'd kept a diary of the month I been there. Only nobody would believe it." The reader learns that he stayed in Miami, but "I guess we drove up to Palm Beach one night. I don't know" (SC, 441). The meals were probably fine though he usually didn't eat any. He went out to look at some property, but it was too hard to see without any moon. Fretts, like the other Florida visitors in Lardner's stories, had soon established a routine. "It was the same schedule, day after day, the whole time I was there. The party would start out along about seven, eight o'clock in the evening and go to whatever place we hadn't been the night before. We'd dance till, say, one o'clock and then chase the women home and do a little serious gambling. The poker game generally broke up a little before noon. That would give us fellows the afternoon to sleep, w'ile the girls would do their shoppin' or go to the polo or waste their time some way another. About six o'clock,

I'd get up and have the barber come in and shave me and then I'd dress and be all set for the roll-call." Fretts never had time for golf or tennis or fishing. "Fishing! That's a whole day!" (*SC,* 443–44).

When Walters says the weather was beautiful, Fretts responds, "So I heard somebody say." Fretts has spent an entire month doing exactly what he had been guilty of in New York—drinking, gambling, and carousing. But he concludes: "After this, I'm going to take all my vacations in the winter and spend them right there. That's the Garden Spot of God's Green Footstool!" (*SC,* 442). Convinced that his Florida vacation has done him a world of good, he returns home "sun cured."

If "Gullible's Travels" had poked fun at the social climbers and "The Golden Honeymoon" had spoofed the elderly pleasure-seekers, "Sun Cured" was Lardner's satire on the frenetic businessman who went to Florida to escape the rat race but took the rat race with him, or, more correctly, joined the ensuing one in Miami where the land boom was reaching its wildest heights before the crash.

For each of these characters Florida represents a dream, be it access to the social scene, rejuvenation at a quiet resort, or the retreat from the everyday rat race. For each the dream is elusive. The Gullibles do not achieve social success, the honeymooners almost have their marriage wrecked, and Fretts has probably raised his blood pressure even more. In each of these stories Lardner creates with his Florida settings a might-be place in which dreams may be realized but usually are not. In "Sun Cured" the picture is harshest; Fretts does not even partake of the beautiful surroundings.

America of the 1920s, characterized by rootlessness, frenetic pace, scrambling for the dollar to ensure social mobility, was carefully chronicled by Ring Lardner—first with his pictures of the Busher and later and most completely with his dream-chasing characters who saw in Florida the epitome of all they were after, pleasure in one of its many forms. High-toned Palm Beach, St. Petersburg of the golden agers, or Miami with its night life—each was used imaginatively by Lardner in his fiction to catch the pulse of American life in the twenties.

Lardner never wrote the Great American Novel that his supporters had hoped for. Edmund Wilson's query—"Will Ring Lardner, then, go on to his *Huckleberry Finn* or has he already told all he knows?"—must be answered this way: Lardner had told more than many of the critics realized.[15] Perhaps Lardner disappointed his friends, but the man who was generally so taciturn that he was described by a friend in 1922 as "Rameses II, with his wrappings off," had communicated a great deal.[16] In his sketches of the American boob, his stories of middle America, he showed Americans still pursuing their elusive dreams, still looking for that Eden that would make their fondest wishes come true. Americans needed such an Eden, and in the 1920s Florida still held out a promise of fulfilling one's dream of restored health or hedonistic pleasure. If its promise was not always fulfilled, it seemed nevertheless as close as one might come.

15 Edmund Wilson, *A Literary Chronicle: 1920–1950* (Garden City, N.Y., 1956), 40.
16 Evans, *Ring Lardner*, 3.

V
The Last Wild Country

> *The launch rolled in the Gulf Stream swell and Harry Morgan lay on his back in the cockpit. At first he tried to brace himself against the roll with his good hand. Then he lay quietly and took it.*
> —Ernest Hemingway
> To Have and Have Not

In April of 1928 a young writer returning from his years as an expatriate in Europe arrived by ship in Key West harbor. Ernest Hemingway, already renowned for his fiction, had come with his new wife, Pauline Pfeiffer, for what was to be a stay of six weeks or so before deciding upon a place of residence in America. It took only a few days of exploring the town, its beaches, its bars, its opportunities for deep sea fishing, to capture Hemingway's admiration for the place. Key West was remotely situated sixty miles from mainland Florida, and its population had dwindled to only twelve thousand from the boom times of the mid-twenties. The planned visit of a few weeks led to a number of lengthy stays and finally to the purchase of a house where Hemingway did some of his best writing. Key West was to become the setting for *To Have and Have Not*, his only novel based in America. When Hemingway finally made a complete break from Key West in 1940, it was to move one hundred miles south to Cuba in hopes of regaining those very things that had appealed to him in Key West.

For what Hemingway found in Florida was a wild, tropical place that was still largely unfettered by the entrapments of civilized everyday life. Hemingway's Florida was a place where a man could match himself against the elements in contests with the great marlin, a place where someone daring enough could run whiskey for handsome profits. In this Florida one could find the freedom largely lacking in the rest of the country, the freedom to live and thrive according to the tenets of one's own code. Only in the 1930s, when the government in the form of the Works Progress Administration and other projects began to interfere with Florida as he knew it, did Hemingway strike out for new territory.

The appeal of Key West to Hemingway's imagination is understandable. Given its relative isolation, the cosmopolitan qualities of Key West were remarkable. As one chronicler of the town notes: "The history of Key West dates back to Indians, Spanish explorers, conquistadors and pirates. Because of its strategic location, the island became a melting pot. Lighthearted Cubans mingled with Bahamian seamen. New England sea captains, merchants, and aristocratic southerners rubbed elbows to create a unique island culture."[1]

Key West had reached its boom period after the completion of Henry Flagler's overseas railroad in 1912 when the population grew to almost twenty thousand. The town continued to thrive as a military center during World War I. With the end of the war, Key West suffered a number of economic losses: "the armed forces were

[1] Jim Brasher, "Hemingway's Florida," *Lost Generation Journal*, I (1973), 4.

moved away; the cigar factories had departed to Tampa and sponge fishing was taken over by the divers from Tarpon Springs."[2]

When Hemingway arrived in Key West the town had not yet plunged to its economic depths. After the collapse of the Florida boom and the onset of the depression, a number of residents moved away. By 1933 a fourth of the population was on relief, and the following year the community was placed in the hands of the Federal Emergency Relief Administration, which planned to rebuild the town into a resort. Volunteers, including artists who created murals on buildings throughout the town, worked to refurbish Key West into a tourist center, but a major setback occurred when the hurricane of September, 1935, destroyed parts of the overseas railroad and killed almost five hundred war veterans who lived in three Civilian Conservation Corps camps on the Keys. Hemingway was among those who searched for bodies, and believing, as did many others, that the veterans' deaths could have been avoided by more efficient warnings of the impending hurricane, he wrote a scathing article protesting their deaths.

Key West did not begin to thrive in an economic way again until the Overseas Highway, built in part on the remaining railroad pilings, was completed in 1938, opening the town again as a tourist center. As James McLendon has noted, "Even before the 1935 hurricane the New Deal was heavily committed to the Keys." The government "meant to rebuild them; they meant to help the people and they did. But to the hardy Conchs and to artists like Hemingway the changes would be hard to accept." With the completion of the Overseas Highway and the building of federal housing projects, "the island charm was on the wane. Middle-class America was on its way to Key West after more than a hundred years."[3] And for Hemingway it was time to light out for the territory again.

How Hemingway made his way to Key West has been amply documented. Probably no other American writer has had his life so

---

2 Dovell, *Florida*, II, 810.
3 James McLendon, *Papa: Hemingway in Key West* (Miami, Fla., 1972), 138–39.

thoroughly explored and written about as has Hemingway. Not only have the details of his life spawned a cult of hero-worshipers, but the biographical fallacies have become a major obstacle to the interpretation of his work. As Louis D. Rubin, Jr., has noted, "Once we are familiar with Hemingway, we tend to regard all of his fiction as extensions of his personality."[4] What is important here is to determine what drew Hemingway to Key West and how he used both the setting and the protagonist, Harry Morgan of *To Have and Have Not*, to tell a story about Florida—and America.

To trace Hemingway's career before he settled in Key West and wrote *To Have and Have Not* is to realize some striking parallels with his fellow writers who preceded him to Florida. The similarities with Ring Lardner have been noted—growing up in a small midwestern town, striking out at a young age into a writing career. Philip Young has also pointed out the parallels with Stephen Crane. They both "began very young their careers as reporters, and quickly became foreign correspondents. They traveled widely, and to the same places: Key West, the American West and Cuba; Europe, a Greco-Turkish War, and so on." Although Hemingway later repudiated Lardner's influence, he acknowledged his indebtedness to Crane, seeing in "The Open Boat" Crane's concern with style and with the relationship between man and his environment.[5]

Although they seem an unlikely pair for comparison, Hemingway and Henry James also share similar qualities. Hugh Holman notes that Hemingway "is most like James for he left America without leaving Americans; in large measure he deserted the American scene in his major works . . . but he made his subject in part the American abroad." Holman also notes the two share a "singleminded devotion to . . . craft."[6] Most important for this study, however, is the fact that both writers, returning to America from Europe, found in Florida what they would use symbolically as the

4 Louis D. Rubin, Jr., "The Self Recaptured," *Kenyon Review*, XXV (1963), 412.
5 Philip Young, *Ernest Hemingway*, (New York, 1952), 162, 164.
6 C. Hugh Holman, "Ernest Hemingway," in "Modern Novelists and Contemporary American Society: A Symposium," *Shenandoah*, X (Winter, 1959), 5.

heart and soul of America. For James six days in Florida was sufficient; in contrast, Hemingway's visit to Florida turned into a stay of some twelve years.

Hemingway had already conquered Europe, married, divorced, and married a second time before he returned to America in 1928. In Key West he and his second wife, Pauline, rented an apartment. The colorful setting and history of Key West, which lies approximately 120 miles out to sea, only 90 miles from Cuba and 150 miles away from the Bahamas, instantly appealed to him. When Hemingway arrived, Key West had been linked to the mainland by Henry Flagler's railroad for only sixteen years. The Overseas Highway would not be built for some years.

In his study of Hemingway's years in Key West, James McLendon argues that "the single most important chunk of the author's life has been passed over and almost obscured to date." Referring to the twelve years from 1928 to 1940 that Hemingway spent as a "permanent or sometime resident," McLendon says that in the "strange cosmopolitan backwater" of Key West, "with its almost mystical island presence, he found what he was to become." Dos Passos, who visited Hemingway several times, was also to sense the faraway quality of the place that he described as "something seen in a dream."[7]

Alfred Kazin has also commented on the special qualities of Hemingway's newfound home.

> Like the Paris of 1925, Key West is at once an outpost of a culture and its symbol. It is a home for disabled and unemployed veterans, a night resort for writers who talk great books, a harbor for the sleek yachts of the newer millionaires. Being a tip of the continent, it is an open door to Cuba, a window on the Gulf Stream, the Florida of the boom all over again, albeit a little tarnished; and a bit of Latin America. It is by Key West that Hemingway went home, and it is Key West, apparently, that remains America in cross-section to him; the noisy, shabby, deeply moving rancor and

7 McLendon, *Papa*, 16, 20.

tumult of all those human wrecks, the fishermen and the Cuban revolutionaries, the veterans and the alcoholics, the gilt-edged snobs and the hungry natives, the great white stretch of beach promising everything and leading nowhere.[8]

After several moves, Hemingway and Pauline established a permanent home on Whitehead Street. They restored a large, run-down house, built the first swimming pool in Key West, and equipped a study for the writer on the second floor of the old carriage house. Hemingway was not amused when the Whitehead Street house was designated as stop number eighteen on a list prepared by the tourist board of forty-eight things to see in Key West. One of his favorite stories was that he kept an aged black man out front to impersonate him and run off tourists.[9] If he was frustrated by the affronts to his privacy, he continued to be taken with the charms of the town, and later, when he felt Key West was growing too large, he nevertheless could effectively describe the lure of its surroundings.

In the first place, the Gulf Stream and the other great ocean currents are the last wild country there is left. Once you are out of sight of land and of the other boats you are more alone than you can ever be hunting and the sea is the same as it has been since before men ever went on it in boats. In a season fishing you will see it oily flat as the becalmed galleons saw it while they drifted to the westward; white-capped with a fresh breeze as they saw it running with the trades. . . . The Gulf Stream is an unexploited country.[10]

Key West meant many things to Hemingway. Although it was far from an urban center, its cosmopolitan qualities appealed to the re-

8 Alfred Kazin, "Hemingway's First Book on His Own People," in Robert O. Stephens (ed.), *Ernest Hemingway: The Critical Reception* (New York, 1977), 175.
9 Ernest Hemingway, "The Sights of Whitehead Street: A Key West Letter," in William White (ed.), *By-Line: Ernest Hemingway: Selected Articles and Dispatches of Four Decades* (New York, 1967), 192.
10 Ernest Hemingway, "On the Blue Water: A Gulf Stream Letter," in White (ed.), *By-Line*, 237–38.

cent expatriate. At the same time its relative isolation from the mainstream of life afforded him the privacy necessary for his work. When he finished his daily writing stint, there were plenty of pleasures to indulge in—swimming with friends, drinking at Sloppy Joe's Bar, fishing in the Gulf all the way to Cuba.

More important than these things, Key West sparked Hemingway's imagination. As Kazin has noted, Key West, in many ways, represented the best and worst in America. On one hand Key West with its juxtaposition of down-and-out veterans and poor fishermen with wealthy yacht owners showed America of the thirties—the depression years when the great contrasts between the haves and have-nots were accentuated. In Key West there were natives, known as Conchs, who could hardly make enough money to feed their families. Only a few hundred yards away in their yachts in the harbor were the idle rich that Lardner had poked fun at in his stories. When Hemingway came to write about the latter group of people he would, as Lardner had done, show them desperately seeking happiness and rarely finding it.

But if Key West showed the misery of the thirties, it nevertheless retained many of the paradisic qualities that had drawn so many people to it in the first place. The temperate climate, beautiful ocean vistas, and most important to Hemingway, the lawlessness, including smuggling tax-free rum even after Prohibition had ended, that prevailed there were highly appealing. Key West natives had their own standards of government, and because of its remote location, there was in Hemingway's time (and still to a great degree today) a primitive, frontier quality to the place. Hemingway had referred to the Gulf Stream as an unspoiled place; to a large extent, Key West was still a place where a man could live by his own code and people would not trouble him about it.

Although Hemingway treated the Keys in several magazine articles and one story, his most sustained treatment came in the book that was to arouse much controversy, *To Have and Have Not*. Probably the harshest criticism of the novel was that of Delmore Schwartz. "*To*

Have and Have Not is a stupid and foolish book, a disgrace to a good writer, a book which should never have been printed." A more balanced assessment is Alfred Kazin's review in which he found the novel "feverishly brilliant, and flat by turns."[11]

To determine what Hemingway did well in *To Have and Have Not* it is necessary first to consider what he did wrong. As Carlos Baker observed, "Hemingway himself once described [the novel] . . . as a procedural error—an attempt, that is, to make a novel out of what ought to have remained a novelette about a Key West soldier of fortune named Harry Morgan." Instead of doing this, Hemingway worked off and on at the book for three or four years. The Morgan episodes were "first conceived and first written as three short stories." The first, "One Trip Across," published in 1934, introduces Harry Morgan, "ex-policeman from Miami, charter-boat fisherman out of Key West, a proud and independent man who took to smuggling as a means of supporting his wife and daughters in lieu of letting them go on relief." The second Harry Morgan story, written in 1935 and entitled "The Tradesman's Return," has Harry losing his right arm to gunfire and having his boat confiscated after bringing over illegal liquor from Cuba. Hemingway, as Baker notes, had decided to flesh out these stories into a novel. Taking the material with him to Wyoming, he worked on a third Morgan story and a companion story in which he introduced the young Richard Gordon, a failed writer, and his friends. Richard Gordon, his wife, and the smart social set were to be used as a foil for the simple, hardworking Harry Morgan and his blowsy but loving wife, Marie, a former prostitute.[12]

It is an overstatement to say, as did one critic, that the only unity

---

11 Delmore Schwartz, "Ernest Hemingway's Literary Situation," in John K. M. McCaffery (ed.), *Ernest Hemingway: The Man and His Work* (New York, 1969), 123; Kazin, "Hemingway's First Book on His Own People," in Stephens (ed.), *Ernest Hemingway: The Critical Reception*, 174.

12 Carlos Baker, *Hemingway: The Writer as Artist* (4th ed.; Princeton, 1972), xv–xvi, 203–204.

in *To Have and Have Not* is in the binding, but certainly Hemingway's plan for the book, which looked good on paper, did not work out.[13] The final result is an awkward yoking together of segments: there is the Harry Morgan story, the central plot of the book; the Richard Gordon story, with its sneering comments on the failed writer who looks for "quaintness" in faraway Key West and misunderstands everything he sees; and finally there is the roll call of the yachts at the conclusion of the novel in which Hemingway condemns the empty life of the rich—the homosexual rich boy who will soon commit suicide, the nymphomaniac woman whose lover ignores her, and so on.

As Baker notes in his able analysis of *To Have and Have Not*: "The assumption in [the novel] was that Depressed America at large could be anatomized by using a microscope on Key West in little. America at its worst was fully visible in Key West during the period 1932–36." A noble plan, but artistically one that, for Hemingway at least, simply did not work. The story of Richard Gordon, meant to heighten the Harry Morgan story and to throw "Harry Morgan's masculine virtue into bolder relief," generally adds nothing to the Morgan story.[14] Additionally, the long concluding section on the yachts with its shifts in point of view from the have nots to the haves contains some of Hemingway's blandest writing. The wealthy people on the boats are merely caricatures of people; they are so cardboardlike that they fail to sustain the reader's interest. If *To Have and Have Not* was one of Hemingway's rare attempts, as some critics have said, to write a novel of social protest, it failed both thematically (the message was undercut by the weakness of the characters he was using to illustrate his points) and artistically (the juxtaposition of the thesis material distorted what was in itself an exciting, well-fashioned story—the tale of Harry Morgan).

Almost all of what does succeed in *To Have and Have Not*, then, is

---

13 William James Ryan, "Uses of Irony in *To Have and Have Not*," *Modern Fiction Studies*, XIV (Autumn, 1968), 329.

14 Baker, *Hemingway: The Writer as Artist*, 206, 204–205.

related to the story of Morgan's life and death struggles. Harry's story grows out of that other aspect of Key West that Hemingway found there—the last frontier, a place where there was still room for heroes.

As with almost every aspect of *To Have and Have Not*, a critical controversy has continued over whether Harry Morgan is hero or villain; is he a man who does the wrong things for the right reasons, or is he a murderous, evil renegade? This much seems clear: from the outset of the story Harry Morgan is a doomed man, betrayed by the social and economic conditions of his life.

We are first introduced to Morgan in a bar in Havana where after turning down a handsome offer of money for smuggling Cubans to the Keys, he sees them gunned down on the sidewalk outside the cafe. Harry has said that he does not like to smuggle anything that can talk. Returning to his boat, Harry takes Mr. Johnson, a wealthy businessman from the States, out on the final day of three weeks of fishing. Morgan's analysis of Johnson is an unflattering one. Johnson loses a marlin that "a fisherman would give a year to tie into . . . he loses my heavy tackle, he makes a fool of himself and he sits there perfectly content, drinking with a rummy" (*THHN*, 22). If Johnson is a fool, he is also morally corrupt; for after promising to pay Harry the $825 he owes him on the next day, he takes a plane to Miami. Morgan and his mate, Eddy the rummy, are left in Havana with not even enough money to buy fuel for the trip back to Key West.

Only because Harry is without money does he then strike a deal with a Chinaman, Mr. Sing, to transport a dozen Chinese to the Keys. Assured by Sing that it does not matter where he drops them and knowing that Sing, a broker, wants only the money and has no concern for the lives of the refugees, Harry accepts the money, then after the Chinese are transferred to his boat, kills Sing and dumps the Chinese back on shore. His justification for this act is that he killed Sing "to keep from killing twelve other Chinese" (*THHN*, 55). He returns to Key West with $1200, enough to support Marie and their daughters for the summer.

In Part Two of the novel Harry is smuggling liquor up to the Keys because "the depression had put charter boat fishing on the bum" (*THHN*, 85). When he and his black mate Wesley are pursued and Wesley is shot in the leg and Harry wounded in the arm, Harry pulls the boat up close to shore on one of the outer Keys, and with his one good arm begins to toss the liquor overboard. In this scene the Key West code is clearly apparent. Another fisherman, Captain Willie, who has chartered his boat to a party of visitors, sees Morgan's boat. When his party tells Captain Willie to go alongside, he refuses. "If he wanted us he would have signalled us. If he don't want us it's none of our business. Down here everybody aims to mind their own business" (*THHN*, 79). The visitor, Frederick Harrison, tells the captain that he is "one of the three most important men in the United States today" and orders Willie to approach the boat, to which the captain responds, asking him if he is so important, "What the hell you doing in Key West, then?" The captain then calls out to Harry, "I got a guy here on board some kind of stool from Washington. More important than the President, he says. . . . He thinks you're a bootlegger. He's got the numbers of the boat. I ain't never seen you so I don't know who you are. . . . I don't know where this place is where I seen you. I wouldn't know how to get back here" (*THHN*, 80, 83).

Like Johnson, Harrison is another outsider, a violator of the code. Another indication of his inability to appreciate the value of Key West is found in his remark, "Fishing is nonsense. . . . If you catch a sailfish what do you do with it?" (*THHN*, 82). Harrison has no understanding of the importance of the ritual that takes place in the struggle, just as he has no appreciation of the code of life Hemingway is writing about.

As Part Two closes, Harry, having lost his liquor and fearing that his boat will be confiscated by the Coast Guard, worries about his wound. "I hope they can fix that arm. . . . I got a lot of use for that arm" (*THHN*, 87). In the beginning of Part Three, Harry, now one-armed, is in Freddy's Bar making arrangements to smuggle some Cuban revolutionaries back to Havana. His confiscated boat is tied up in the harbor, but he plans to steal it. He enlists the help of

Albert, a friend of his who is now working on relief earning $7.50 a week digging up sewer lines. Harry's sermon to Al sums up the economic situation in Key West and justifies Harry's illegal smuggling activities. "Look at me. I used to make thirty-five dollars a day right through the season taking people out fishing. Now I get shot and lose an arm, and my boat, running a lousy load of liquor that's worth hardly as much as my boat. But let me tell you, my kids ain't going to have their bellies hurt and I ain't going to dig sewers for the government for less money than will feed them. . . . they're trying to . . . starve you Conchs out of here so they can burn down the shacks and put up apartments and make this a tourist town. . . . they're buying up lots, and then after the poor people are starved out and gone somewhere else to starve some more they're going to come in and make it into a beauty spot for tourists" (*THHN*, 96).

Albert, who is the narrator of this section of Part Three, reflects on Harry. "When he was in a boat he always felt good and without his boat he felt plenty bad. I think he was glad of an excuse to steal her" (*THHN*, 97). Although Harry rescues his boat, its hiding place is discovered, and desperate to earn some money, he hires the *Queen Conch* owned by Freddy but does not tell him the real reason for using it. Having rendezvoused with the revolutionaries after they have robbed a bank to finance their revolutionary activities, he soon realizes the full extent of the danger he is in. In these final scenes Harry's (and perhaps Hemingway's) ambivalence about the revolution is reflected. The Cubans kill Albert so that he cannot talk, and one of the Cubans explains to Harry that Albert's murderer "is a good revolutionary but a bad man. . . . He kills in a good cause, of course. The best cause" (*THHN*, 158). Harry muses to himself, "To help the working man he robs a bank and kills a fellow works with him and then kills that poor damned Albert that never did any harm. That's a working man he kills" (*THHN*, 168).

Harry knows he must kill the Cubans before they murder him. "He had abandoned anger, hatred and any dignity as luxuries, now, and had started to plan" (*THHN*, 159). He shoots the Cubans, but one of them wounds him in the stomach. In the final scene with

Harry, the Coast Guard tows in the *Queen Conch* and a crowd gathers in the harbor to see it brought in. "The crowd was as quiet as only a Key West crowd can be" (*THHN*, 227). At the conclusion of the novel, Marie, grieving for the loss of her husband, returns home, and in a book in which there is remarkably little description of the lush surroundings, the author leaves the reader with this little coda after Morgan's death: "Outside it was a lovely, cool, sub-tropical winter day and the palm branches were sawing in the light north wind. . . . In the big yard of the house across the street a peacock squawked. Through the window you could see the sea looking hard and new and blue in the winter light" (*THHN*, 261–62). Here the wildness and freedom and beauty of Key West are figured as an appropriate setting for the life and death of Harry Morgan.

For those critics who see *To Have and Have Not* as a complete failure, the death of Harry Morgan is nothing more than the sordid end of a smuggler. But as Baker and others have noted, Harry Morgan's life can be seen as much more. Given the context of his setting and his faithful adherence to his own code of ethics, Harry Morgan is a tragic hero.

Both Leo Gurko and Philip Young have not missed the point that Harry's namesake was Henry Morgan, "the pirate, who once ravaged the coasts off which Harry works, who like Harry was really hard, but brave and resourceful too." As Young accurately observes, "Where the parallel breaks down, we get what may be the main point of it; following his capture by the law Henry was knighted; Harry was killed."[15]

Not only did Hemingway provide Harry with a special antecedent; it is not difficult to see Harry as "a lineal descendent of the American frontiersman, the man who made his own laws and trusted in his own judgments. . . . Both in the Far West and in Key West Hemingway had met men of the frontier temperament, so that he did not lack for contemporary models." Baker concludes, "there

---

15 Young, *Ernest Hemingway*, 43–44. See also Leo Gurko, *Ernest Hemingway and the Pursuit of Heroism* (New York, 1968), 149.

is no difficulty in taking Morgan as the type of the old, self-reliant individualist confronted by an ever-encroaching social restraint."[16] For restraint is precisely what Harry Morgan encounters, as Richard Lehan notes. "Hemingway explicitly contrasts the elemental man with a sick society that destroys him, and this novel is Hemingway's most expressed attack on America and modern culture."[17] Unlike his predecessors who could always move on, time and place had run out for Harry. "Huck Finn could always light out for the territory when things got too uncomfortable at home. In Harry Morgan's time there was no territory to light out for. He managed to escape from the settled, overcrowded earth to water, but even the free expanse of water was no longer free. Every country in the Caribbean had coast-guard cutters, chopping up the sea in controllable segments, boxing in those who sought to maneuver on their own."[18] Betrayed by capitalists, and governments, Harry has no chance for victory, except perhaps in death. And in typical Hemingway fashion, he accepts death stoically. To the people on the yachts who witness Harry's boat being towed in he is nothing but another dead Conch, but to the perceptive reader Harry Morgan, through his adherence to the code of individuality, has lived by it and died by it, nobly.

Harry Morgan was squeezed out of his paradise at last by the encroachment of institutions and people. But in his depiction of Harry, Hemingway portrayed some of Key West's finest elements. For a time at least Key West was one of the few outposts in America where the frontier spirit survived.

Like Harry Morgan, Hemingway loved the individualistic spirit of Key West. The breakup of his second marriage and the building of the Overseas Highway to the Keys were both factors in bringing an end to his enjoyment of the easy pace of life there. With Key West closed to him, he would turn to Cuba, the Bahamas, and the Gulf

16 Baker, *Hemingway: The Writer as Artist*, 210–11.
17 Richard Lehan, "Hemingway Among the Moderns," in Richard Astro and Jackson J. Benson (eds.), *Hemingway in Our Time* (Corvallis, 1974), 202.
18 Gurko, *Ernest Hemingway and the Pursuit of Heroism*, 148.

Stream itself for the final works, *The Old Man and the Sea* and the posthumously published *Islands in the Stream*. But the Key West interlude had been an important one for Hemingway. He did some of his best writing there (*A Farewell to Arms*) and though *To Have and Have Not* falls short of being one of his best works, the character of Harry Morgan epitomized perhaps one of the last American heroes who could still live, for a time at least, by an individualistic, primitive code.

As Leo Gurko has noted, during the time Hemingway was in Key West the depression "toppled the businessman as the reigning god in the American pantheon and substituted the idea of collective action for the early pioneer idea of individual free enterprise. But at the height of the depression there was a period when the old order was cracking up while the new one was not yet in sight."[19] Key West reflected this change, even though some individuals resisted it. Harry Morgan scrambled to live by his own individualistic code even as the effects of the depression robbed him of his livelihood, and finally his life.

In his portrayal of Florida in *To Have and Have Not*, Hemingway showed what had seemed a paradise, a holdout against bourgeois American life, at the very moment when it would have to succumb, to a degree at least, to the forces of the depression that were controlling the rest of America. And it is precisely because this southern outpost of Florida was being threatened that its primitive qualities remained so important in Hemingway's vision. This wild, primitive place, so isolated that it maintained its own individualistic code into the early decades of the twentieth-century industrial age, remained for Hemingway the heart of what America had once been and had now lost. Although fast disappearing, it was the last wild country.

19 *Ibid.*, 143.

VI
An Enchantment Slightly Sinister

> Cross Creek belongs to the wind
> and the rain, to the sun and the
> seasons, to the cosmic secrecy of
> seed, and beyond all, to time.
> —Marjorie Kinnan Rawlings
> Cross Creek

It was in the same year that Hemingway went to Key West that a young writer who thus far had had little luck in publishing her fiction made a visit to Florida. Marjorie Kinnan Rawlings, married only a few years and struggling to find herself as a writer, was so intrigued by her first impressions of central Florida that in 1928 she and her husband left their home and work in Rochester, New York, and bought seventy-four acres south of Gainesville, Florida, at Cross Creek.[1] Charles Rawlings eventually tired of

---

1 Gordon E. Bigelow, *Frontier Eden: The Literary Career of Marjorie Kinnan Rawlings* (Gainesville, Fla., 1966), 3–4.

the charms of rural life in Cross Creek, but after their divorce Marjorie Rawlings stayed on. "For myself," she would write later, "the creek satisfies a thing that had gone hungry and unfed since childhood days. . . . after long years of spiritual homelessness, of nostalgia, here is that mystic loveliness of childhood. Here's home. An old thread, long tangled, comes straight again" (CC, 5, 7-8).

Marjorie Rawlings found at Cross Creek something akin to what Thoreau had realized at Walden Pond. Although Rawlings' Florida was not a garden of Eden—it was replete with ants, skunks, and snakes—it was, nevertheless, a place where one could live in close accord with nature, attuned to the changes of the seasons, in complete harmony with the surroundings. For Rawlings life at the orange grove at Cross Creek was as close to an idyllic life as is possible on earth. Her Florida of groves, scrub, and rivers was a largely unspoiled paradise.

Even though some of her writing treats other places, Rawlings is best known as a Florida writer. She spent her childhood in Washington, D.C., where she was born in 1896. In 1918 she graduated from the University of Wisconsin. She married Charles Rawlings in 1919, and while living in Rochester, New York, worked on short fiction, which never found a publisher. It was only after her move to Florida and her discovery of the wealth of material for the literary imagination that she found her true element for fiction. As Gordon Bigelow notes, "Her mature life and literary career can be understood only in terms of her discovery of Florida in 1928, and this was for her as much as for Ponce de Leon four centuries earlier, a true discovery."[2] By 1930 she had sold her first Florida story, "Cracker Chidlings," to *Scribner's*, and other stories followed quickly.

With the Florida setting providing the inspiration she had needed in her work, she published rapidly. In 1933, the novel *South Moon Under* appeared. *The Golden Apples* followed in 1935. In 1938 came her greatest critical and popular success, *The Yearling*. Other Florida works include a short story collection, *When the Whippoorwill* (1940),

2 Ibid., 2.

and *Cross Creek* (1942). Later in her life Rawlings decided to write a novel based on her grandfather's life, *The Sojourner* (1953). But the book, which was poorly received, fell far short of her Florida writing. Perhaps Rawlings, who died in 1953 at Crescent Beach, Florida, felt she had exhausted the material of her surroundings, but it is clear that it was Florida that had struck her imagination and had provided the raw materials for her best work.

The Yearling is Rawlings' best-known work, but *Cross Creek* offers her richest portrayal of the Florida setting. *Cross Creek*, which has been called a Florida *Walden*, fixes upon the Eden-like qualities of a tiny hamlet in north-central Florida. In the opening chapter Rawlings states that her sojourn at Cross Creek is not so much an escape from life as it is a return to a source of spiritual renewal. Settling down to live in a simple house surrounded by an orange grove, she found a richer life than the one she had left behind. "I am often lonely," she says in *Cross Creek*, "but I should be lonelier in the heart of a city" (CC, 5).

Rawlings struggled with the structure of *Cross Creek*, which is essentially a series of portraits of the people she knew and an account of her experiences while living in the cracker farmhouse. The opening chapter, "For This Is an Enchanted Land," reflects the idyllic tone of the entire work that is reiterated in the final chapter, "Who Owns Cross Creek?" The answer is that, in truth, no one can own a paradise. The other twenty chapters are loosely connected, with the exception of four chapters treating each of the seasons. The overall effect is to create of Cross Creek a garden of Eden, a place in which there are occasional serpents, but in which harmony and beauty generally prevail.

Throughout *Cross Creek* there is a strong sense of the peaceful coexistence of the various inhabitants. Blacks and whites need one another, as Rawlings illustrates in her account of her neighbor Martha Mickens. "When old Martha Mickens shall march at last through the walls of Jericho . . . a dark rock at the core of the Creek life will have been shattered to bits. She is nurse to any of us, black or white, who fall ill. She is midwife and layer out of the dead. She is the only one who gives advice to all of us impartially. She is a dusky Fate, spinning away at the threads of our Creek existence" (CC, 17). Martha also expresses the eternal qualities of Cross Creek. "They's been fine folks here . . . and they's been trash. But Sugar, the grove ain't trash, and the Creek be's trashified here and there, but it's the Creek right on" (CC, 20).

In *Cross Creek* Rawlings frequently uses the orange grove as symbol of enchantment.

> Any grove or any wood is a fine thing to see. . . . It is necessary to leave the impersonal highway, to step inside the rusty gate and close it behind. By this, an act of faith is committed, through which one accepts blindly the communion cup of beauty. One is now inside the grove, out of one world and in the mysterious heart of another. Enchantment lies in different things for each of us. For me, it is in this: to step out of the bright sunlight into the shade of orange trees; to walk under the arched canopy of their jadelike leaves; to see the long aisles of lichened trunks stretch ahead in a geometric rhythm; to feel the mystery of a seclusion that yet has shafts of light striking through it. This is the essence of an ancient and secret magic. It goes back, perhaps, to the fairy tales of childhood . . . to all half-luminous places that pleased the imagination as a child. . . . And after long years of spiritual homelessness, of nostalgia, here is that mystic loveliness of childhood. (CC, 7–8)

Like Thoreau, Rawlings notes the differences among the seasons in her world, finding that in Florida the changes, though less marked, are very special. "Here in Florida the seasons move in and out like nuns in soft clothing, making no rustle in their passing" (CC, 243). In the chapter "Summer," Rawlings perhaps best captures the essence of the grove. "I have lain on my veranda and asked no more of the summer day than to watch, one by one, the lotus petals falling" (CC, 269). She points out, though, that winter at Cross Creek also has a special beauty. When a freeze threatens the grove, the people light fires to protect the fruit trees. "The smoke lifts from the fires gray-white, melting into gray-blue, drifting like the veils of a dancer

An Enchantment Slightly Sinister / 111

under the open skies. Each orange tree is outlined with light. The green leaves shine like jade. The round golden oranges are each lit with a secret inner candle. My heart bursts with the loveliness of the grove at night" (CC, 336).

In "Hyacinth Drift," the next-to-last chapter in *Cross Creek*, Rawlings recounts a trip down the St. Johns River that is reminiscent of Bartram's voyages. Suffering from the breakup of her first marriage, Rawlings and her friend Dessie decide on a river trip as a cure. Although the two women are discouraged from traveling alone, they set out near the headwaters of the river for a journey of several hundred miles. Rawlings carefully recounts the sights and sounds of the river, the marshes of the headwaters, the false channels. As it was for Bartram, Rawlings' voyage on the river is like a trip to one's spiritual source. "If I could have, to hold forever, one brief place and time of beauty, I think I might choose the night on that high lonely bank above the St. John's River. . . . Suddenly the soft night turned silver. . . . We lay on our cots a long time wakeful because of beauty. . . . There was a deserted grove somewhere behind the cabin, and the incredible sweetness of orange bloom drifted across us" (CC, 350–51).

In her concluding chapter, Rawlings asks, "Who owns Cross Creek?" Her answer appears earlier in the book where she implies that no one owns it. "Florida has survived the West Indian hurricanes that brush our coast. . . . It has maintained against all enemies its beauty, and at such places as the Creek, its privacy" (CC, 282). Cross Creek can be enjoyed, it can be lived in, but it cannot be possessed. The elusiveness that Rawlings pictures as she describes Cross Creek suggests that though in one sense Cross Creek is a real place, in another sense it is a mythical place as well. Reading *Cross Creek* one shares with Rawlings the sense of the initiate who is ushered into a might-be land. Reading on a literal level, one finds that her descriptions are perhaps too good to be true. As Gordon Bigelow notes of Rawlings' treatment of Martha Mickens, "Aunt Martha was in real life a pleasant and handsome elderly woman with an alert mind and warm, engaging personality who was wise in many ways with the wisdom of age, but she was by no means the sage nor the aristocratic social arbiter of the local Negro community which Marjorie represents her as being."[3] But taken figuratively these descriptions become for the reader, as for Rawlings, a counterpoint to the life in the North she had left behind her. The publishing success of *Cross Creek* shows that the book made an imaginative appeal to its readers far beyond that of a travelogue account of a northern woman's experience in an orange grove. *Cross Creek* appeals to anyone who has longed for an idyllic, pastoral escape from a humdrum life. In her picture of Cross Creek as a veritable paradise Rawlings echoed for twentieth-century readers those same enchanting qualities that had appealed to Americans for so many years.

Rawlings' circle of friends in Florida came to include fellow writer James Branch Cabell, who wintered regularly in St. Augustine after 1935 and who later dedicated one of his Florida-based books to Rawlings and another to her second husband, Norton Baskin. Although Rawlings and Cabell were friends and admirers of one another's work, no two writers could have differed more in the ways in which they transformed into literature their impressions of Florida in the 1930s and 1940s. Rawlings was a realist who concentrated on the accurate depiction of the land and plants, the birds and animals, as well as the black and white inhabitants of rural Florida. Although she was capable of manipulating her material into fiction and essays, her techniques were not really that far removed from those of William Bartram, who had also used an abundance of realistic detail as the basis of his paeans to Florida. In contrast, Cabell in his trilogy, *It Happened in Florida*, began with real places and real people, but noted of his own work that it treated "persons who, in the manner of gargoyles, have figured with a grotesque prominence in Florida's well-nigh uniformly fantastic chronicle" (*DDS*, xii). In his writing Cabell takes Florida to new literary dimensions. Realism is out entirely as Cabell creates of Florida an absolute fantasy.

3 *Ibid.*, 142.

For Cabell it was not so much the Florida that really existed that was important; for that matter, he took pleasure in poking fun at the tourist industry that was re-creating history in St. Augustine to make it more easily accessible to visitors. Cabell, however, also re-created Florida's past in his writing in order to create a mythical Florida that was even better than the reality, where the old Ponce de León Hotel in St. Augustine could become a cloud castle of one's dreams. Cabell's Florida might be peopled with ordinary citizens, but among them also walked the dashing pirates of older times and even a few fallen angels who bestowed magical gifts upon a lucky few. In Cabell's Florida extraordinary things could happen.

Although James Branch Cabell became a good friend to Marjorie Rawlings, to many other people he was an enigma. "There are more arguments to prove that James Branch Cabell is a legend than to prove that he is a fact," wrote Carl Van Doren in an early, impressionistic study of the quiet man who was to shock the literary world with his "obscene" novel, *Jurgen*.[4] Born into an aristocratic Virginia family, longtime friend of fellow writer Ellen Glasgow, Cabell seemed an unlikely candidate to stir up controversy. Yet as later biographers have shown, there was from his early life on an aptitude in Cabell for trouble, beginning with a scandal in college (an investigation cleared him of any wrongdoing) and continuing with rumors implicating him in the murder of a cousin. The greatest uproar in Cabell's life was the court trial centering on the obscenity in *Jurgen*, which had the effect of catapulting its author to national prominence.

Just as he had been quickly thrust into the national limelight, Cabell faded rather swiftly from it. Frank Durham's essay on him entitled "The Author Who Died Twice," reflects Cabell's eclipse. "Those of us in our forties and fifties who read him avidly in the dear, dead days hadn't thought of him in so long that it came as a shock to hear that he had died in May, 1958." But James Branch Cabell had continued to write long after his national preeminence had faded. After 1935 he suffered from periodic bouts with pneu-

---

4 Carl Van Doren, *James Branch Cabell* (New York, 1932), 1.

monia and began spending winters in St. Augustine. As Joe Lee Davis notes, "Cabell's own past and the legendry and history of both Virginia and Florida came more and more to absorb his attention."[5] Although he still spent time in Virginia, less in Richmond now and more at his summer home at Northern Neck, his winters in Florida and his interest in St. Augustine gave impetus to much of his later writing. In addition to biographical works and Virginia-based fiction, his later work included a trilogy, *It Happened in Florida*, made up of three works published in the 1940s. Although there seems to be a critical consensus that the later works add little to what Cabell had said in *The Biography of Manuel* (the eighteen volumes, the most famous of which is *Jurgen*, set in the imaginary land of Poictesme), they are still worth considering, for not only do they continue some of the same themes developed by Cabell in *The Biography of Manuel*, they demonstrate how he could in his last trilogy make imaginative use of Florida, as he had of Virginia, and thus fashion what is certainly one of the richest and most fanciful pictures of Florida ever to appear in fiction.

Although not much has been written about Cabell's later work, dozens of critics have offered their interpretations of *The Biography of Manuel*. The antics of Jurgen and the faraway qualities of Poictesme have been duly viewed and reviewed. Often praised as an impeccable stylist, Cabell has generally been considered a writer of escapist literature, and Jurgen's search for youth is cited as evidence of the escapist qualities of Cabell's fiction. Louis D. Rubin, Jr., has successfully argued that Cabell was not escaping the South in his fiction.[6] Poictesme, far from being Cabell's rejection of his native setting, is a mythical place in which the same problems that confront us in daily life confront Cabell's characters. Additionally, it is wrong to view daily life and the mythmaking process as mutually ex-

[5] Frank Durham, "The Author Who Died Twice: James Branch Cabell," *Georgia Review*, XVI (Spring, 1962), 163; Joe Lee Davis, *James Branch Cabell*, (New York, 1962), 25–26, 40.

[6] Louis D. Rubin, Jr., *No Place on Earth: Ellen Glasgow, James Branch Cabell, and Richmond-in-Virginia* (Austin, 1959), 56 ff.

clusive. Virginians of Cabell's time were busily re-creating their war heroes, casting them into larger-than-life fashion. What Cabell chose to do in his fiction was not to escape from the reality of everyday life but to create a new stage in which his characters could come to terms with the universal, age-old problems of life and death, youth and age, love and hate. It is not surprising that Jurgen in Poictesme finally makes the compromise that all of us must make in our own lives.

As Rubin notes, "First and foremost . . . is the magic journey into the supernatural, which always ends not in escape and contentment, but in the decision to return home to mortal compromises and the known limitations of existence."[7] Given his preoccupation with mythmaking and its relationship to everyday life, it is not surprising that Cabell's Florida experiences fired his imagination. Here was a spot of earth that from its first discovery by white men had been linked with myth and the quest for supernatural powers. And here was Cabell, making annual winter visits in, if not mundane, certainly ordinary tourist quarters, who could use those myths and larger-than-life figures and work them into what would turn out again to be, as in the chronicles of Poictesme, a comment on the choices, circumstances, and compromises of everyday life. One might have predicted that the hero of Cabell's last work of fiction, *The Devil's Own Dear Son* (1947), upon discovering that his real father was Red Samaël, the most lecherous of all the devils of hell, would return from a visit to hell and be content with his father's gift of an oil circulator and a new coat of paint for the family-owned tourist home.

Cabell's first work based entirely in Florida was a *tour de force*, a fanciful account of the history of the St. Johns River on which he collaborated with Rollins professor A. J. Hanna, and which was published in the Rivers of America Series under the general editorship of Stephen Vincent Benét. The working relationship between the two authors was clearly set out in a letter from Cabell to Hanna of May 4, 1941. "I propose that, after being formally empowered to

7 Ibid., 73.

do a book on the St. Johns, you are to construct it out of the scholarship and the knowledge I lack, and I—well, stylize it as pungently as I can manage."[8]

Although the two worked together successfully, Cabell was to remark to Burton Rascoe two years later that the book was "an interesting but mind wrecking job. I am still sincerely fond of my colleague, but I had never imagined that any professor could be quite so meticulously professorial . . . we wrangled over every paragraph; but the result is, the more thanks to Hanna, a sound and valuable book." Their major difference was that as a historian Hanna was attempting an accurate account of the long history of the St. Johns. On the other hand, Cabell would, as he remarked to Hanna, "decline to consider the book as a history. It is an account of various persons who have lived beside the St. Johns."[9]

Working with Hanna's facts in *The St. Johns*, Cabell managed to recreate the figures who had lived beside the river, blending their mythic qualities with their human foibles. The result is a three-hundred-page account of what one reviewer has called a "history of an altogether new and transcendent kind, in which facts are made to read like fiction and textbook mummies are reincarnated in all their original addiction to wine, women, and song." Marjorie Kinnan Rawlings succinctly praised his work. "Mr. Cabell has dallied along the banks and up a few irreverent and bawdy byways but the course of the book flows as steadily as the river."[10]

That the St. Johns would be considered as no ordinary river is apparent in the initial description. "Neither the Mississippi nor the Nile exceeds the average expanse of the St. Johns between shore to shore for a full hundred miles above its mouth" (*SJ*, 3–4). The

---

8 James Branch Cabell to A. J. Hanna, May 4, 1941, in Edward Wagenknecht (ed.), *The Letters of James Branch Cabell* (Norman, 1975), 203.

9 *Ibid.*, 108, 209.

10 Stetson Kennedy, Review of Branch Cabell and A. J. Hanna's *The St. Johns*, in *New York Times Book Review*, September 5, 1943, p. 7; Marjorie Kinnan Rawlings, Review of Branch Cabell and A. J. Hanna's *The St. Johns*, in *New York Herald Tribune Weekly Book Review*, September 5, 1943, p. 3.

following twenty-nine chapters recount the history of the river and the figures who have lived, loved, and fought beside it with, from the outset, a hint that both good and evil have lurked about it, "the forces of an enchantment just slightly sinister" (*SJ*, 8).

The early history of the river is as colorful as the characters associated with it. Jean Ribault, the Frenchman who landed in 1562 at the River of May, as he called it, lavishly praised it. "His accounts of the semifabulous fairyland surrounding his newly discovered huge river so cordially aroused the concern of English empire builders that by-and-by his fervent descriptions were printed. . . . and were thus made available for such highly cultured persons as could read" (*SJ*, 22). The following chapters sum up the various battles of France, Spain, and England for possession of the Florida territory, giving a tongue-in-cheek perspective of the Indian inhabitants. "You could not ever convince any one of [the Europeans] that your country did not abound with gold mines and silver mines and enormous pearl fisheries" (*SJ*, 45). Henry James had waxed eloquent on the Spanish fort at St. Augustine. Cabell was also to describe the fort, especially the dungeons "in which a vast number of Englishmen were to have the tedium of their imprisonment varied by refinements of torture" (*SJ*, 73).

In the early accounts of Florida it is noted of the St. Johns that "of the natural wealth . . . of all Florida, divers printed accounts, no one . . . appears to have been disfigured by understatement" (*SJ*, 89). After this tongue-in-cheek historical treatment, Cabell did not hesitate to parody the literary figures and others who wrote about Florida. Calling William Bartram the "ne'er-do-well son of a fairly famous botanist," he speculates on the influence of Bartram's descriptions on the English romantic movement, saying that "the romantics all dipped into Bartram's *Travels* prehensilely" (*SJ*, 101, 108).

Sidney Lanier is criticized in *The St. Johns* as writing "not inexcusably, but even so, with a lushness of diction such as one has learned more ordinarily to associate with the prattling elder poets of New England" (*SJ*, 15). Harriet Beecher Stowe is cited for her promotional writing. "Howsoever incoherently Mrs. Stowe may have injured the South some twenty years earlier, now her surprising paeans as to the 'lapis lazuli blue colored' St. Johns, and as to the semitropical paradise called Florida—even though quite as loosely based upon facts as had been *Uncle Tom's Cabin* . . .—did result in an immediate and a most profitable increase of tourist travel from out of the North" (*SJ*, 232–33). Cabell later defended his remarks on the domestic harmony of the Stowe household in a letter to Burton Rascoe. "All the Stowe data . . . is true, and she utters nothing which is not taken from her correspondence; what the captain says is more freely inventive. But his plight harried me when I thought about anybody's having to live in the same house with Harriet Beecher Stowe."[11]

Near the end of *The St. Johns* is an account of the demise of the river as a main tourist area when Henry Flagler developed the railroad on the state's east coast and Henry Plant built one on the west. "The railroads of both these northern invaders then combined to make bankrupt the steamboat lines and the tourist traffic of the St. Johns" (*SJ*, 273).

The most controversial chapter of the book is the last one, containing the tale of Cora Crane in which her life after Stephen Crane's death, including the building of a new house of pleasure, the Court, modeled after Brede Manor, is satirically recounted. As if to soften the concluding tone of the work, the epilogue contains an imaginary dialogue between the two collaborators in which Hanna remarks, "I do not approve of the flippant liberties which have been taken in the Stowe chapter." Cabell responds, "So let us end our book, instead, not quite with Cora Crane's story, since you resent its sordidness, but rather with an elaborated prose passage . . . dwelling upon the ephemeral nature of worldly glory" (*SJ*, 289, 291).

There follows an idealized description by Hanna of the beach at Mt. Cornelia to which Cabell responds, "I also have visited Mt. Cornelia, where, I admit, not every one of these reflections occurred to

11 James Branch Cabell to Burton Rascoe, September 18, 1943, in Wagenknecht (ed.), *The Letters of James Branch Cabell*, 108.

me." This hint at the blend of myth and reality, idealism and debunking, that characterizes *The St. Johns* is summed up in the concluding vision where again the reference is made to "enchantment . . . slightly sinister" (*SJ*, 292). *The St. Johns* is finally neither history nor fiction but a culmination of both. Having yoked the protesting Professor Hanna into his fanciful portrait of the St. Johns, Cabell would soon proceed on his own to spin even more fantastic visions of Florida.

In the novel *There Were Two Pirates*, the second work of the trilogy, Cabell narrowed his focus to a single figure, José Gasparilla, king of the pirates, who operated off the coast of West Florida in the latter part of the eighteenth century. An editorial note asserts that the book is an edited version of Gasparilla's autobiography. There follows an account of Gasparilla's birth in Spain, his rise to power, his parting from his beloved childhood sweetheart Isabel as he sails to America promising his return when he has earned 500,000 pesos.

Gasparilla's careful treatment of his conscience as he undertakes a career of murdering for booty is explained this way: "As my first formal act in office [as a self-appointed ruler], I herewith declare war against all other existing governments; so that by every one of you these oncoming homicides may be attended to with an unstained conscience, as being patriotic necessities directed against the enemies of our way of living" (*TP*, 11–12). Gasparilla describes his first act of piracy but forbears to recount the others—"One sea-fight is much like another." As the years pass he has a number of mistresses who are kept in a grand style at his home base on the islands off Tampa Bay. "But at all times my heart remained faithful to Isabel" (*TP*, 18, 25).

Although Cabell had greatly embellished the legend of Gasparilla, the first two parts of the novel are somewhat faithful to the Gasparilla story. As part three begins, however, Cabell unfolds a plot that veers quickly into fantasy while seeming remarkably familiar to readers of his earlier works.

While robbing a ship carrying Don Diego de Arredondo, Gasparilla discovers that Don Diego's wife is none other than his beloved Isabel, who after seven years of marriage has become a fat, homely housewife with a brood of five children. Later, by means of the mysterious powers of a green stone in Don Diego's watch fob, Gasparilla is sent for nine years to the land of shadows where he is reborn and again falls in love with the little Isabel. Returning from the land of dreams he discovers that his shadow has been carrying on his pirating business for him with great success. Gasparilla marries the now-widowed Isabel and is a happy stepfather to her children—now there are six of them, including a little stepdaughter who would figure prominently in the final book of the trilogy. We learn that Gasparilla did not die in Tampa in 1821, as legend has it, but some eight years later in St. Augustine. Gasparilla is pleased to let his shadow carry on for him and lives openly in St. Augustine where he bores his companions with dull stories about his close relative, the pirate Gasparilla.

Just as Jurgen had forsaken youth and returned home to his dowdy wife, Gasparilla finds happiness with the plump, middle-aged Isabel. But in *There Were Two Pirates* Cabell takes his protagonist one step farther, for here Gasparilla exists in two forms: the bold pirate and the quiet little man content with his domestic life. Not every man can have it both ways, but Gasparilla can as he lives in St. Augustine with Isabel and also follows the exploits of his shadow successor.

In *There Were Two Pirates* Cabell has taken one of Florida's heroes, embellished upon his legend, and with characteristic Cabellian irony, turned him into everyman—the man who has dreams but must finally accept compromises. Placing the mundane choices of everyday life against a fabulous setting of exotic coastal islands and buccaneer ships, Cabell has created a fantasy destined to appeal to the imagination of every reader who has dreamed of an escape from ordinary life.

An even more fantastic story is that of *The Devil's Own Dear Son: A Comedy of the Fatted Calf*, the last of Cabell's Florida trilogy and his most comprehensive treatment of the enchantments, both idyllic and sinister, of Florida. In the preface to the novel Cabell gives his version of how he chose St. Augustine as a wintering place. Riding through "the sedately green Plaza of St. Augustine, which at the instant was interpenetrated and gold-washed by the sunlight of a superb afternoon, I became enamored, subconsciously, when I passed through it" (*DDS*, xii). In St. Augustine as he knew it in the thirties and forties, he places the hero of his last work, a young man, Diego de Arredondo Dodd, a relative of the Isabel we met in *There Were Two Pirates*. Diego's life starts out mundanely enough; his parents are proprietors of the Bide-A-While Tourist Home, which his mother denigrates daily. Born an Arredondo, she feels her husband "ought to be running the Pedro Menendez de Aviles Guest House, with a coat of arms out in front of it" (*DDS*, 5).

As Diego approaches manhood, his parents expect him to marry and take over the tourist home, but he has other plans. "I have need to be going to and fro in the earth, and to be walking up and down in it" (*DDS*, 13). He decides that he will see the world, make his fortune, come back and marry his childhood sweetheart, Catherine Mary. They will then tear down the tourist home and build a castle like the Ponce De León Hotel, only much handsomer.

Diego fails, of course, in his quest for glory. Returning to St. Augustine he finds his mother has died, his father looks more content, and Catherine Mary has married, divorced, and grown fatter. At this point the bildungsroman plot takes an unusual turn. Just as Diego is settling into middle-class St. Augustine life, joining the Rotary Club and so forth, he learns that the white-haired old man he has always thought was his father is not his father at all. The elder Dodd tells Diego that he appeared at his birth as a fire coming down the chimney with a little green stone in his hand. His great aunt Isabel tells him the rest of the story, that his mother's lover had been Red Samaël, the only one of the seventy princes of darkness who was cursed with the fire of eternal youth.

What follows is Diego's journey to the underworld in search of his real father. Riding a horse that used to romp in Poictesme, he enters a castle "remarkably like the lobby of the Ponce De León hotel" where he meets his father and sees a vision of himself and the young Catherine Mary. Rejecting the idle dreams of his youth, Diego leaves the castle that these dreams "had builded, and with which Diego had no longer any vital concern" (*DDS*, 152, 170).

Awakening in the peaceful Huguenot cemetery with its trees draped with Spanish moss, Diego, still in the company of Red Samaël, "wondered, mildly, that in any surroundings thus beautiful and so sedative, his father should still be speaking in a tone of lively dissatisfaction. But then young people were like that, always" (*DDS*, 177). Red Samaël offers his son wealth, power, and, the most precious gift of all, renewed youth. The wish Diego finally asks for, though, is an oil-circulator and a new coat of paint for the tourist home. And Diego, fearing that he might be tempted to again call on his father and ask for his youth again, casts the green stone into Matanzas Bay.

Just as Jurgen and Gasparilla ventured into the supernatural and returned, Diego too discovers that the true object of his quest lies not in another world but at his own hearth. No longer does he dream of castles; the Bide-A-While with its fresh coat of cream-colored paint and brilliant red roof and trim will satisfy his needs.

In *The Devil's Own Dear Son* Cabell, beginning with the rather ordinary daily life of visitors and residents of St. Augustine, builds a fabulous tale of seduction by devils; of a highway described as "not differ[ing] from the state highways of . . . Florida" lined by billboards attempting to lure the damned to territories beyond an overcrowded, no-vacancies hell; of green stones that give power; of the possibilities of eternal youth. The richest product of Cabell's imaginative treatment of Florida, *The Devil's Own Dear Son* becomes the ultimate statement of Florida as fantasy.

In Cabell's work, Poictesme was not really so far from Richmond-in-Virginia. The same human foibles, the same choices and compromises were found in both places. Through Poictesme Cabell was able to make a comment on the condition of modern life. The same is true in his use of the legends and other mythical qualities of Florida. The boon of eternal youth, long associated with Florida's legend, can be granted by Red Samaël, but Diego rejects it. Fabulous golden treasure, also said to be in Florida, is within Gasparilla's grasp; indeed, he has buried treasure all over the state. But in Cabell's revised version of his life, he rejects the gold for a quiet life with Isabel.

Florida offered Cabell in his middle age a fertile source for new tales, new quests into the world of dreams. Much like his characters in Poictesme, his Florida characters finally chose to come to terms with their own everyday lives. In this sense, the Florida trilogy is not unlike Cabell's earlier work, extending familiar themes into new territory. In Cabell's work, Florida is raised to the highest levels of fantasy. Here, perhaps for the first time, the fantastic legends and myths that were at the root of Florida's history all along are incorporated into a literature equally fantastic. Cabell created a vision of Florida that spoke to the very heart of the American imagination.

VII
The Single Artificer of the World

> As the immense dew of Florida
> Brings forth hymn and hymn
> From the beholder,
> ....
> So, in me, come flinging
> Forms, flames, and the flakes of
>   flames.
>   —Wallace Stevens
>   "Nomad Exquisite"

When he made his first trip to Florida in 1916, Wallace Stevens was immediately struck by a place and climate unlike any he had ever known as a boy in Pennsylvania and as a young attorney in New York. As a representative of the Hartford Accident and Indemnity Company, Stevens made frequent business trips to the South and to Florida for thirty years. But the fact that his trips were for business reasons in no way interfered with Stevens' recognition of the imaginative possibilities of Florida. He called Florida "one of the most delightful places I have ever seen." In 1922 he wrote of Key West, "The place is a paradise—midsummer weather, the sky brilliantly clear and intensely blue, the sea blue and green beyond what you have ever seen," and in the following year he quoted a traveling companion that in Florida "we are drowned in beauty."[1]

Another letter he wrote in 1930 from Key West is reminiscent of the earlier musings of Harriet Beecher Stowe as she basked in the sun at Mandarin. "I have been down here actually for a week but it seems as if I had never been anywhere else and never particularly wanted to be anywhere else at least for some considerable time to come." As Miami developed more and more into a tourist mecca and Key West became "furiously literary" in the 1930s, Wallace Stevens regretted the changes that were taking place, though he found that one could still find unspoiled places in Florida in which the beauties of nature still predominated. The most revealing letter Stevens wrote concerning Florida, though, and one in which the poet's own relationship with it was defined, was to Samuel French Morse in 1943. "My particular Florida shrinks from anything like Miami Beach. In any case, unless your mind is made up, you may find that you have picked up an individual Florida of your own which will keep coming back to you long after you are back home. I used to find the place violently affective."[2]

It was Stevens the businessman who made the trips to Florida, often accompanied by his friend Judge Arthur Powell, with whom he did not discuss poetry. But it was Stevens the poet who transformed his Florida experiences into some of the most complex symbols and metaphors ever created of American life in the twentieth century. In 1935 he wrote, "I have been going to Florida for twenty years, and all of the Florida poems have actual backgrounds."[3] The twenty or so poems based in Florida are, however, much more than

---

1 Wallace Stevens to Elsie Stevens, April 21, 1916, January 10, 1922, January 30, 1923, in Holly Stevens (ed.), *Letters of Wallace Stevens* (New York, 1966), 192, 225, 233.
2 Wallace Stevens to James A. Powers, February 19, 1930, Wallace Stevens to Samuel French Morse, May 27, 1943, in *Ibid.*, 258, 449–50.
3 Wallace Stevens to Ronald Lane Latimer, October 31, 1935, in *Ibid.*, 289.

local-color descriptions. As a group they re-create the journey of the modern everyman to a primitive, sensual world which he may ultimately reject, but which he can never entirely forget. Wallace Stevens' Florida, which is pictured in sensuous, realistic detail, is also, and more importantly, a Florida of the mind. For the images of Florida that William Bartram had recorded so faithfully would become in Stevens' poetry symbols for the highest form of reality, the reality of the imagination.

Born in 1879, Stevens first visited Florida when he was in his late thirties. His first volume of poetry, *Harmonium*, published in 1923, contains his fullest treatment of Florida, but Florida is also a subject in his second work, *Ideas of Order* (1936). Although Florida was never mentioned in his poetry after *Ideas of Order*, the same themes of which Florida was so integral a part were continued throughout his writing until his death in 1955. For Stevens, the Florida experience was a major factor in his literary development.

Randall Jarrell once remarked of Stevens' first volume of poetry that "there has never been a travel poster like *Harmonium*."[4] One of Stevens' most written-about works, *Harmonium* has been called both a young man's gaudy excesses in poetry and his most brilliantly conceived and executed verse. Critics who admire the vibrant imagery and exotic settings of *Harmonium* find his later work too cerebral. Others, however, find the more introspective verse of *Parts of a World* and other later works to be more mature in the rejection of the gaudy imagery of *Harmonium*.

Among the many analyses of *Harmonium* is one by Jan Pinkerton who places Stevens in the tradition of Hawthorne, Melville, and Henry Adams as a "participant in a unique nineteenth-century American tradition of conservative protest. . . . all of these men, like Stevens, dreamed to varying degrees of the exotic and forbidden—and all of them nevertheless felt ultimately secure only in their own less threatening culture." The tropics, says Pinkerton, "provided an imaginative alternative to the destructive, acquisitive

---

4 Randall Jarrell, *Poetry and the Age* (London, 1955), 124.

course which they felt America was taking." Noting that the image of the tropics was not so much real as it was a northern fantasy, Pinkerton says that "in Stevens we have perhaps the last complete working out of this pattern: the journey South to protest the ills of one's society and the return North to rest secure once more in the only culture in which one could find peace." In *Harmonium* Stevens would praise the tropics, and in Florida "he had seen much and had rid himself of much." Having done so, he could "return to the North, where 'reality' is barer, where it is reduced to more fundamental colors and forms, and where he [could] devote the major body of his poetry not to tropical scenes but to a more difficult, more tortuous attempt to grasp 'reality.'"[5]

Pinkerton is one among a number of critics who have argued that the Florida poems of *Harmonium* and *Ideas of Order* chronicle Stevens' early infatuation and later rejection of Florida in his life and work. Stevens' use of the Florida material, however, is far more complex than a simple love-hate affair. What is more important is that out of his Florida experience Stevens developed a complex symbol for his preoccupation with the relationship between reality and the imagination. A survey of his poetry reveals that in the early poems, especially those of *Harmonium*, he is intrigued with the lush, sensual imagery that Florida affords and that figures so richly in the poetry. Even in these early poems, however, there is a sense of being overwhelmed by the richness of nature, a hint that there is, within this fecund world, a threat to the poet's ability to control, to order his material.

In *Ideas of Order* Stevens takes leave of Florida only to return to it intermittently, but in a different way. In this second volume of poetry Stevens purports to reject the overwhelming sensual reality of Florida to return to the cold North, a place conducive to the cerebral life of the poet, but ultimately he returns to Florida, this time in the mind. In "The Idea of Order at Key West" Florida is used at last in a

5 Jan Pinkerton, "Wallace Stevens in the Tropics: A Conservative Protest," *Yale Review*, LX (December, 1970), 215–16, 221, 227.

more complex way than ever before as a symbol for the imagination. One of Stevens' first Florida poems in *Harmonium*, "Fabliau of Florida," exemplifies his early use of the lush imagery of the semitropics.

> Barque of phosphor
> On the palmy beach,
>
> Move outward into heaven,
> Into the alabasters
> And night blues.

Into the paradisic picture, however, enters a chiaroscuro that remains attractive but with a hint of something less than idyllic.

> Foam and cloud are one.
> Sultry moon-monsters
> Are dissolving.
>
> Fill your black hull
> with white moonlight.

It is in the last two lines of the poem that the ambivalence of the poet toward his subject is undeniable.

> There will never be an end
> To this droning of the surf.
>   (CP, 23)

Here the word *droning* evokes a sameness that, in spite of the beauty of the ocean, is ominous. The same idea would be reiterated in "Sunday Morning" where an ever-perfect paradise becomes, finally, tedious.

A more elaborate and complex use of semitropical imagery is found in "The Comedian as the Letter C." Herbert Stern has compared this poem to "Farewell to Florida," written fourteen years later, in its concern "with the poet's determination, at once exultant and bitter, to abandon an environment that attracts him because it provides in reality the opulence the imagination craves." In this poem Crispin is an everyman who moves from east to west (from old world to new) and south to north, passing through the Yucatan northward and finally settling in the Carolinas. Joseph N. Riddel notes, "The exotic middle of the voyage provides a revealing interlude, in which the primitive strategy to avoid formlessness (and hence the direct question of origins) is to retreat into set rituals (sonnets which, like myths, structuralize change), another form of colony making."[6]

Crispin ultimately forms a colony in the Carolinas where he will raise four daughters, and, though in a new world, will retain and revive the values he brought with him from the old one. Crispin has sailed away from the Yucatan, much like Stevens had taken leave of Florida; for in a place where the lushness of the surroundings exceeds even the wildest projection of the imagination, one's creative powers may come to nothing.

At the conclusion of "The Comedian as the Letter C" when Crispin has reached Carolina, the speaker wonders

if Crispin is a profitless Philosopher, beginning with a green
    brag,
Concluding fadedly, if as a man
Prone to distemper he abates in taste.

There is a risk in leaving the "green brag" behind, and again the ambivalence of the poet is reflected here.

Of all the poems in *Harmonium* the one that most strikingly juxtaposes images of attraction and repulsion is "O Florida, Venereal Soil." Just as venereal may refer to love or disease or both, so does the poem contain both the beautiful and the horrible.

A few things for themselves,
Convolvulus and coral,
Buzzards and live-moss,
Tiestas from the keys,

---

6 Herbert J. Stern, *Wallace Stevens: Art of Uncertainty* (Ann Arbor, 1966), 151; Joseph N. Riddel, "Stevens on Imagination—The Point of Departure," in O. B. Hardison, Jr. (ed.), *The Quest for Imagination: Essays in Twentieth-Century Aesthetic Criticism* (Cleveland, 1971), 66–67.

> A few things for themselves,
> Florida, venereal soil,
> Disclose to the lover.

The effect of the poem is to lure while at the same time hinting of evil. These conflicting images also appear in the last stanza, in which Florida is figured as a woman, both saintly and seductive.

> Donna, donna, dark,
> ....
> Conceal yourself or disclose
> Fewest things to the lover—
> A hand that bears a thick-leaved fruit,
> A pungent bloom against your shade.
> (CP, 47-48)

Florida is an Eden, but it is also a paradise in which temptation and destruction are imminent.

Although no direct reference to Florida is made in what is perhaps Stevens' best-known poem, "Sunday Morning," the lushness and indolence so typical of the Florida settings pervade the poem. In the realization of the woman of the poem that "Death is the mother of beauty" is found Stevens' harshest criticism of the imperishable bliss of the tropics. Stevens had noted how in Florida the seasons did not change. In "Sunday Morning" the question is asked,

> Is there no change of death in paradise?
> Does ripe fruit never fall? Or do the boughs
> Hang always heavy in that perfect sky.
> (CP, 69)

Although there was certainly death and decay in Florida, there was, for the most part, ever-present foliage, green and lush. Crispin had to leave such a climate before it stifled him. The woman in "Sunday Morning" can also feel no contentment in the thought of an unchanging paradise.

"Nomad Exquisite" is one of Stevens' fullest descriptions of the poet's relationship with his surroundings.

As the immense dew of Florida
Brings forth
The big-finned palm
And green vine angering for life,

As the immense dew of Florida
Brings forth hymn and hymn
From the beholder,
Beholding all those green sides
And gold sides of green sides,

And blessed mornings,
Meet for the eye of the young alligator,
And lightning colors
So, in me, come flinging
Forms, flames, and the flakes of flames.
                    (*CP*, 95)

Here Stevens creates a consciousness not at odds with its surroundings but coequal. "As the immense dew of Florida" creates, so does the "I" of the poem "come flinging / Forms, flames, and the flakes of flames." If fire here connotes the imaginative spark of man, in this one poem at least, nature is conducive to creativity.

"Indian River" sounds a different note.

> The trade-wind jingles the rings in the nets around the racks by the docks on Indian River.
> It is the same jingle of the water among the roots under the banks of the palmettoes,
> It is the same jingle of the red-bird breasting the orange-trees out of the cedars.
> Yet there is no spring in Florida, neither in boskage perdu, nor on the nunnery beaches.
>   (*CP*, 112)

In this poem the lush descriptions evoke images of sameness, of sterility of much the same kind as those in "Sunday Morning." The redbird's song is the "same jingle." The repetitive sound of the trade wind, the water, and the bird's song reflect the sameness of seasons—a point that Rawlings commented on in *Cross Creek* in which she took issue with Stevens' complaint. Stevens, in a letter to his wife in January of 1919, had noted that a winter day in Miami "is a heavenly change; but our rich variety of four seasons, our Exquisite Spring and long autumn give us a variety that the lotus-eaters of the South must pine for."[7]

Stevens' ambivalence toward Florida that evoked the complex imagery of his poetry was continued in his second volume, *Ideas of Order*, which was published thirteen years after *Harmonium*. When *Ideas of Order* was first published in a limited edition the opening poem was "Sailing After Lunch." In the trade edition that followed, however, Stevens substituted "Farewell to Florida," which was to be an elaborate leave-taking of Florida and all that it meant to him.

I

Go on, high ship, since now, upon the shore,
The snake has left its skin upon the floor.
Key West sank downward under massive clouds
And silvers and greens spread over the sea. The moon
Is at the mast-head and the past is dead.
Her mind will never speak to me again.
I am free. High above the mast the moon
Rides clear of her mind and the waves make a refrain
Of this: that the snake has shed its skin upon
The floor. Go on through the darkness. The waves fly back.

II

Her mind had bound me round. The palms were hot
As if I lived in ashen ground, as if
The leaves in which the wind kept up its sound
From my North of cold whistled in a sepulchral South,
Her South of pine and coral and coraline sea,
Her home, not mine, in the ever-freshened Keys,
Her days, her oceanic nights, calling
For music, for whispering from the reefs.

---

[7] Wallace Stevens to Elsie Stevens, January 17, 1919, in Stevens (ed.), *Letters of Wallace Stevens*, 211.

How content I shall be in the North to which I sail
And to feel sure and to forget the bleaching sand . . .

III

I hated the weathery yawl from which the pools
Disclosed the sea floor and the wilderness
Of waving weeds. I hated the vivid blooms
Curled over the shadowless hut, the rust and bones,
The trees like bones and the leaves half sand, half sun.
To stand here on the deck in the dark and say
Farewell and to know that that land is forever gone
And that she will not follow in any word
Or look, not ever again in thought, except
That I loved her once . . . Farewell. Go on, high ship.

IV

My North is leafless and lies in a wintry slime
Both of men and clouds, a slime of men in crowds.
The men are moving as the water moves,
This darkened water cloven by sullen swells
Against your sides, then shoving and slithering,
The darkness shattered, turbulent with foam.
To be free again, to return to the violent mind
That is their mind, these men, and that will bind
Me round, carry me, misty deck, carry me
To the cold, go on, high ship, go on, plunge on.

(CP, 117–18)

Although the speaker asserts that he has left it all behind—bleaching sands, vivid blooms—the reader senses that he protests too much. I hate it, he says. Just as Quentin Compson is unconvincing when he protests too much that he does not hate the South, so does the speaker in this poem fail to convince the reader that his rejection is final. The point is especially reinforced in the final stanza, for the destination is "a wintry slime / Both of men and clouds." Although the speaker urges the ship to plunge on, the destination is hardly figured in idyllic or even praiseworthy terms. If the treatment of Florida has been ambivalent, so also is the North a place both attractive and repellent.

The poems cited here show clearly that Stevens' Florida was a complex place that as a symbol was too rich to be dismissed as a phase in the poet's development, the source of gaudy poems for a not-yet-old poet. More accurately, Stevens' perception of Florida as material, as symbol, was great enough to allow him to react to Florida in a variety of ways. James had said that Florida was a "complex of few interweavings." Stevens saw Florida rather as exceedingly rich, first as a lushness that threatened the imagination, and ultimately as a source of material that could be ordered and transformed by the mind into the greater reality of the imagination.

Nowhere is Stevens' imaginative use of Florida more evident than in "The Idea of Order at Key West." Although the poem has been subjected to a variety of interpretations, it is clearly about the dialectic of the creative imagination with nature or reality. The woman in the poem, the singer of the song, creates a greater reality than that of the ocean at Key West.

> She sang beyond the genius of the sea.
> The water never formed to mind or voice,
> Like a body wholly body, fluttering
> Its empty sleeves; and yet its mimic motion
> Made constant cry, caused constantly a cry,
> That was not ours although we understood,
> Inhuman, of the veritable ocean.
>
> The sea was not a mask. No more was she.
> The song and water were not medleyed sound
> Even if what she sang was what she heard,
> Since what she sang was uttered word by word.
> It may be that in all her phrases stirred
> The grinding water and the gasping wind;
> But it was she and not the sea we heard.
>
> For she was the maker of the song she sang.
> The ever-hooded, tragic-gestured sea
> Was merely a place by which she walked to sing.
> Whose spirit is this? we said, because we knew
> It was the spirit that we sought and knew
> That we should ask this often as she sang.

Here is, in its most definitive form, the statement of the poet that there must be more than simply nature.

> If it was only the dark voice of the sea
> That rose, or even colored by many waves;
> If it was only the outer voice of sky
> And cloud, of the sunken coral water-walled,
> However clear, it would have been deep air,
> The heaving speech of air, a summer sound
> Repeated in a summer without end
> And sound alone. But it was more than that,
> More even than her voice, and ours, among
> The meaningless plungings of water and the wind,
> Theatrical distances, bronze shadows heaped
> On high horizons, mountainous atmospheres
> Of sky and sea.

Instead:

> It was her voice that made
> The sky acutest at its vanishing.
> She measured to the hour its solitude.
> She was the single artificer of the world
> In which she sang. And when she sang, the sea,
> Whatever self it had, became the self
> That was her song, for she was the maker. Then we,
> As we beheld her striding there alone,
> Knew that there never was a world for her
> Except the one she sang and, singing, made.

The singer of the song (the poet, the artist, the creative mind) has created a new order.

> Ramon Fernandez, tell me, if you know,
> Why, when the singing ended and we turned
> Toward the town, tell why the glassy lights,
> The lights in the fishing boats at anchor there,
> As the night descended, tilting in the air,
> Mastered the night and portioned out the sea,
> Fixing emblazoned zones and fiery poles,
> Arranging, deepening, enchanting night.

> Oh! Blessed rage for order, pale Ramon,
> The maker's rage to order words of the sea,
> Words of the fragrant portals, dimly-starred,
> And of ourselves and of our origins,
> In ghostlier demarcations, keener sounds.
> (CP, 128–30)

Stevens phrases his conclusion as a question, but he had indeed provided his own answer. The "green brag" is not enough; in his (or her) song the poet must master the night, portion out the sea, must make an imaginative construct of the raw essence around him.

Stevens did not bid a final farewell to Florida. Instead, in "The Idea of Order at Key West" he finally met Florida on his own terms, those not of the dilettante, the voyeur, but of the artist who can order and control the raw material of the senses, fashioning it into art. It was as if Florida had been waiting all these years, through all the explorations, all the tentative catalogings of her charms, all the nonjudgmental praises of her forms to be finally treated for what she is, a complex rich place—complex enough to have appealed for centuries to the imagination of those who dreamed of an enchanted country, yet also a real place, one with thorns and serpents, perhaps more in abundance than the fabled fortunes. For centuries Florida has appealed to the imagination and evoked from it thoughtful, even excellent, writing. In Stevens' work, Florida evokes as a literary response a vision that encompasses both the real and the imagined. Florida is transformed into a pure art form—Stevens' reality of the imagination.

Epilogue

In the half-century since Wallace Stevens made Florida a part of his dialectic between reality and the imagination, Florida has continued to be important both as a real part of the nation and as a source of imaginative appeal. World War II affected Florida much the same way as had the wars preceding it, though on a larger scale. Again thousands of servicemen were sent to Florida for training, and many of them would return to Florida to live after the war ended. Although the war initially had an adverse effect on tourism in Florida, more than five hundred resort hotels were leased by the government for military uses, thus salvaging the state's economy. The Ponce de León, for example, became for a while a Coast Guard indoctrination center. After 1943 tourism again was in full swing, and the economy was also boosted by industrial military installations, especially shipyards. Florida's population has continued to swell from an influx of people seeking what has been called the best winter climate in the United States. The 1950s saw Florida developing from a rural-dominated state to an urban one. Between 1950 and 1983 Florida grew from the twentieth to the seventh largest state in the nation, and still the people come. Perhaps in no other state have the conflicting goals of growth and preservation from destruction of the very natural resources that have attracted people been so apparent as they are in Florida.

At the same time that Florida (in spite of the threat to the state's ecology) has gained an increasingly important place in the economy and technology of the nation, its continued imaginative appeal is much in evidence. Somehow it is not surprising that Florida has played such an important role in space exploration, that it is from Florida that each new American rocket is launched. And it is also in Florida that the largest embodiments of fantasy and technology—Disney World and Epcot—have been created out of the very swamps and barrens of Florida that Henry James despaired of, suggesting that even if Florida the real is finally lost a man-made paradise will take its place.

Although Florida has continued to evoke a literary response—Elizabeth Bishop, Jesse Hill Ford, Harry Crews, among others, have treated Florida in their work—it seems in some ways appropriate that Florida has become even more prominent in the film medium, as in movies like *Midnight Cowboy*. Two hundred years after Bartram succumbed to a vision of this place, the idea of Florida still evokes an imaginative response. The land of Florida remains an enchanted country—a place seductively different from the ordinary, a land where dreams just might come true.

Bibliography

Primary Works

Baker, Carlos, ed. *Ernest Hemingway; Selected Letters, 1917–1961*. New York, 1981.
Bowers, Fredson, ed. *The Works of Stephen Crane*. 10 vols. Charlottesville, 1969–76.
Cabell, James Branch. *As I Remember It: Some Epilogues in Recollection*. New York, 1955.
———. *The Devil's Own Dear Son: A Comedy of the Fatted Calf*. New York, 1949.
———. *The First Gentleman of America: A Comedy of Conquest*. New York, 1942.
———. *Quiet, Please*. Gainesville, Fla., 1952.
———. *There Were Two Pirates: A Comedy of Division*. New York, 1946.
Cabell, Branch, and A. J. Hanna. *The St. Johns: A Parade of Diversities*. New York, 1943.
Emerson, Edward Waldo, and Waldo Emerson Forbes, eds. *Journals of Ralph Waldo Emerson with Annotations*. 10 vols. Boston, 1909.
Emerson, Ralph Waldo. *Society and Solitude*. Cambridge, 1884.
Geismar, Maxwell, ed. *The Ring Lardner Reader*. New York, 1963.
Hemingway, Ernest. *Islands in the Stream*. New York, 1970.
———. *A Moveable Feast*. New York, 1964.
———. *The Old Man and the Sea*. New York, 1952.

———. *To Have and Have Not*. New York, 1937.
———. *Winner Take Nothing*. New York, 1933.
Irving, Washington. *Wolfert's Roost*. Edited by Roberta Rosenberg. Boston, 1979. Vol. XXVII of Richard Dilworth Rust, ed., *The Complete Works of Washington Irving*.
James, Henry. *The American Scene*. 1907; rpr. Bloomington, 1968.
———. *Partial Portraits*. London, 1888.
King, Edward. *The Great South*. Edited by W. Magruder Drake and Robert R. Jones. 1875; rpr. Baton Rouge, 1972.
Lanier, Sidney. *Florida: Its Scenery, Climate, and History*. 1875; rpr. Gainesville, Fla., 1973.
Lardner, Ring W. *Gullible's Travels, Etc.* Chicago, 1965.
———. *How to Write Short Stories [with Samples]*. New York, 1924.
———. *Lose with a Smile*. New York, 1933.
———. *Round Up: The Stories of Ring Lardner*. New York, 1929.
———. *The Story of a Wonder Man: Being the Autobiography of Ring Lardner*. New York, 1927.
Rawlings, Marjorie Kinnan. *Cross Creek*. New York, 1942.
———. Review of *The St. Johns*, by Branch Cabell and A. J. Hanna. *New York Herald Tribune Weekly Book Review*, September 5, 1943, p. 3.
Seldes, Gilbert, ed. *The Portable Ring Lardner*. New York, 1946.
Stevens, Holly, ed. *Letters of Wallace Stevens*. New York, 1966.
Stevens, Wallace. *The Collected Poems of Wallace Stevens*. New York, 1955.
———. *The Necessary Angel: Essays on Reality and the Imagination*. New York, 1951.
———. *Opus Posthumous*. Edited, with introduction, by Samuel French Morse. New York, 1957.
Stowe, Harriet Beecher. *Palmetto-Leaves*. Boston, 1873.
———. *Regional Sketches: New England and Florida*. Edited by John R. Adams. New Haven, 1972.
Van Doren, Mark, ed. *The Travels of William Bartram*. New York, 1928.
Whitman, Albery A. *Not a Man, and Yet a Man*. 1877; rpr. Upper Saddle River, N.J., 1970.
———. *The Rape of Florida*. 1884; rpr. Miami, Fla., 1969.
Woolson, Constance Fenimore. *East Angels*. New York, 1886.

Secondary Works

Adams, John R. *Harriet Beecher Stowe*. New York, 1963.
Adams, Richard P. "Naturalistic Fiction: 'The Open Boat.'" *Tulane Studies in English*, V (1955), 137–46.

Aldridge, John W. *After the Lost Generation: A Critical Study of the Writers of Two Wars*. New York, 1966.
Allen, Gay Wilson. "Sidney Lanier as a Literary Critic." *Philological Quarterly*, XVII (April, 1938), 121–38.
———. *Waldo Emerson: A Biography*. New York, 1981.
Anderson, John Q. "Emerson and Prince Achille Murat." *Boston Public Library Quarterly*, X (1958), 27–37.
———. *The Liberating Gods: Emerson on Poets and Poetry*. Coral Gables, Fla., 1971.
Anderson, Quentin. "Practical and Visionary Americans." *American Scholar*, XLV (Summer, 1976), 405–18.
Astro, Richard, and Jackson J. Benson, eds. *Hemingway in Our Time*. Corvallis, 1974.
Atkins, John. *The Art of Ernest Hemingway: His Work and Personality*. London, 1952.
Auchincloss, Louis. "Henry James's Literary Use of His American Tour (1904)." *South Atlantic Quarterly*, LXXIV (Winter, 1975), 45–52.
Auden, W. H. "Henry James's 'The American Scene.'" *Horizon*, XV (1947), 77–90.
———. Introduction to *The American Scene, Together with Three Essays from "Portraits of Places,"* by Henry James. New York, 1946.
Backman, Melvin. "Death and Birth in Hemingway." In *The Stoic Strain in American Literature: Essays in Honour of Marston LaFrance*, edited by Duane J. MacMillan. Toronto, 1979.
Baird, James. *The Dome and the Rock: Structure in the Poetry of Wallace Stevens*. Baltimore, 1968.
Baker, Carlos. *Ernest Hemingway: A Life Story*. New York, 1969.
———. *Hemingway: The Writer as Artist*. 4th ed. Princeton, 1972.
———, ed. *Hemingway and His Critics: An International Anthology*. New York, 1961.
Baker, Sheridan. *Ernest Hemingway: An Introduction and Interpretation*. New York, 1967.
Beckett, Lucy. *Wallace Stevens*. London, 1974.
Beebe, Maurice, and John Feaster. "Criticism of Ernest Hemingway: A Selected Checklist." *Modern Fiction Studies*, XIV (August, 1968), 337–69.
Bellman, Samuel I. *Marjorie Kinnan Rawlings*. New York, 1974.
Benamou, Michel. *Wallace Stevens and the Symbolist Imagination*. Princeton, 1972.
Bender, Bert. "The Nature and Significance of 'Experience' in 'The Open Boat.'" *Journal of Narrative Technique*, IX (Spring, 1979), 70–80.
Benedict, Clare, ed. *Constance Fenimore Woolson*. London, n.d.

Bigelow, Gordon E. *Frontier Eden: The Literary Career of Marjorie Kinnan Rawlings*. Gainesville, Fla., 1966.
Blessing, Richard Allen. *Wallace Stevens' "Whole Harmonium."* Syracuse, 1970.
Blish, James. "The Long Night of a Virginia Author." *Journal of Modern Literature*, II (1972), 393–405.
Bloom, Harold. *Poetry and Repression: Revisionism from Blake to Stevens*. New Haven, 1976.
———. *Wallace Stevens: The Poems of Our Climate*. Ithaca, 1977.
Borroff, Marie. *Language and the Poet: Verbal Artistry in Frost, Stevens, and Moore*. Chicago, 1979.
Bourne, Edward Gaylord, ed. *Narratives of the Career of Hernando de Soto in the Conquest of Florida, as told by a Knight of Elvas and in a relation by Luys Hernandez de Biedma, factor of the Expedition*. 2 vols. New York, 1922.
Bowen, Elsie Van Buren. "The Gardens of Henry James." Ph.D. dissertation, Tufts University, 1979.
Brasch, James D. "Hemingway's Words: Enduring James's Thoughts." *Modernist Studies: Literature and Culture 1920–1940*, II (1975), 45–51.
Brasher, Jim. "Hemingway's Florida." *Lost Generation Journal*, I (1973), 4–8.
Brawley, Benjamin. *The Negro Genius: A New Appraisal of the Achievement of the American Negro in Literature and the Fine Arts*. 1937; rpr. New York, 1966.
Brewer, Frances Joan. *James Branch Cabell: A Bibliography of his Writings, Biography, and Criticism*. Charlottesville, 1957. Vol. I of Brewer, *James Branch Cabell*. 2 vols.
Brooks, Van Wyck. "Henry James: The American Scene." *Dial*, LXXV (July, 1923), 29–42.
Brown, Ashley, and Robert S. Haller, eds. *The Achievement of Wallace Stevens*. Philadelphia, 1962.
Brown, Ashley. "Landscape into Art: Henry James and John Crowe Ransom." *Sewanee Review*, LXXIX (Spring, 1971), 206–12.
Brown, Charles H. *The Correspondents' War: Journalists in the Spanish-American War*. New York, 1967.
Brown, Merle E. *Wallace Stevens: The Poem as Act*. Detroit, 1970.
Bruccoli, Matthew J., and Richard Layman. *Ring W. Lardner: A Descriptive Bibliography*. Pittsburgh, 1976.
———, eds. *Some Champions: Sketches and Fiction By Ring Lardner*. New York, 1976.
Bryer, Jackson R., ed. *Sixteen Modern American Authors: A Survey of Research and Criticism*. Durham, 1974.

Buchanan, Margaret Gwen. *DuVals of Kentucky and Virginia, 1794–1935: Descendents and Allied Families*. Lynchburg, 1937.
Buck, Doris P. Review of *The Devil's Own Dear Son*, by James Branch Cabell. Richmond *Times Dispatch*, April 10, 1949, p. 11.
Buck, Paul H. *The Road to Reunion, 1865–1900*. Boston, 1937.
Buitenhuis, Peter. *The Grasping Imagination: The American Writings of Henry James*. Toronto, 1970.
Bullock, Florence Haxton. Review of *The First Gentleman of America*, by James Branch Cabell. *New York Herald-Tribune Books*, January 25, 1942, p. 7.
Burtner, William Thomas, Jr. "Ideal and Actual Society: Theme and Technique in Henry James's *The American Scene*." Ph.D. dissertation, Miami University (Oxford, Ohio), 1973.
Burton, Richard. "Review of 'The American Scene.'" *Bellman*, April 20, 1907, p. 476.
Butcher, Fanny. "The Literary Spotlight." Chicago *Tribune*, May 9, 1948, p. 2.
Butcher, Philip. "Emerson and the South." *Phylon*, XVII (Third Quarter, 1956), 279–85.
Butwin, David. "Turning the Keys." *Saturday Review*, February 27, 1971, pp. 38–40.
Cabot, James Elliot. *A Memoir of Ralph Waldo Emerson*. 2 vols. Boston, 1887.
Cady, Edwin H. *Stephen Crane*. Boston, 1980.
Canary, Robert H. *The Cabell Scene*. New York, 1977.
———. "James Branch Cabell and the Comedy of Skeptical Conservatism." *Midcontinental American Studies Journal*, VI (Spring, 1965), 52–60.
Cargill, Oscar. *Intellectual America: Ideas on the March*. New York, 1941.
Caruthers, Clifford M., ed. *Ring Around Max: The Correspondence of Ring Lardner and Max Perkins*. Dekalb, Ill., 1973.
Cobbs, John L. "Hemingway's *To Have and Have Not*: A Casualty of Didactic Revision." *South Atlantic Bulletin*, XLIV (November, 1979), 1–10.
Colum, Padraic, and Margaret Freeman Cabell, eds. *Between Friends: Letters of James Branch Cabell and Others*. New York, 1962.
Colvert, James B. "Style and Meaning in Stephen Crane: *The Open Boat*." *Texas Studies in English*, XXXVII (1958), 34–45.
Conway, Moncure Daniel. *Emerson: At Home and Abroad*. 1883; rpr. New York, 1968.
Cox, Merlin G., and J. E. Dovell. *Florida: From Secession to Space Age*. St. Petersburg, Fla., 1974.

Crane, Milton. "Restoration in St. Augustine." *Saturday Review of Literature*, April 23, 1949, p. 12.
Davis, Joe Lee. *James Branch Cabell*. New York, 1962.
Day, Cyrus. "Stephen Crane and the Ten-foot Dinghy." *Boston University Studies in English*, III (Winter, 1957), 193–213.
Debellis, Jack. *Sidney Lanier*. New York, 1972.
DeMerás, Gonzalo Solis. *Pedro Menéndez de Avilés*. Translated, with notes, by Jeannette Thurber Connor. Gainesville, Fla., 1964.
Dos Passos, John. "Old Hem Was a Sport." *Sports Illustrated*, June 29, 1964, pp. 58–67.
Dovell, J. E. *Florida: Historic, Dramatic, Contemporary*. 4 vols. New York, 1952.
Downes, Alan J. "The Legendary Visit of Emerson to Tallahassee." *Florida Historical Quarterly*, XXXIV (April, 1956), 334–38.
Durham, Frank. "The Author Who Died Twice: James Branch Cabell." *Georgia Review*, XVI (Spring, 1962), 162–68.
Earnest, Ernest. *The Single Vision: The Alienation of American Intellectuals*. New York, 1970.
Eberhart, Richard. "Emerson and Wallace Stevens." *Literary Review*, VII (Autumn, 1963), 51–71.
Edel, Leon. *Henry James: The Middle Years, 1882–1895*. Philadelphia, 1962.
———. "Speaking of Books: Henry James Looked Ahead." *New York Times Book Review*, November 12, 1967, pp. 2, 70–72.
Eder, Doris L. "The Meaning of Wallace Stevens' Two Themes." *Critical Quarterly*, XI (Summer, 1969), 181–90.
———. "Wallace Stevens: Heritage and Influences." *Mosaic*, IV (Fall, 1970), 49–61.
Eddins, Dwight. "Wallace Stevens: America the Primordial." *Modern Language Quarterly*, XXXII (March, 1971), 73–88.
Edwards, C. H., Jr. "Bibliography of Sidney Lanier: 1942–1973." *Bulletin of Bibliography*, XXXI (January–March, 1974), 29–31.
Elder, Donald. *Ring Lardner*. Garden City, N.Y., 1956.
Enck, John J. *Wallace Stevens: Images and Judgments*. Carbondale, 1964.
Evans, Elizabeth. *Ring Lardner*. New York, 1979.
Fairbanks, George R. *History of Florida*. Philadelphia, 1871.
Firestone, Clark B. "River of Variety." *Saturday Review of Literature*, September 11, 1943, p. 7.
Fishwick, Marshall W. "Two Roads from Eden." *Modern Age*, II (Fall, 1958), 404–407.
Fitzgerald, F. Scott. *The Crack-Up*. Edited by Edmund Wilson. New York, 1945.

Foerster, Norman. "Lanier as a Poet of Nature." *Nation*, June 21, 1919, pp. 981–83.
Fox, Frank W. "The Eden World of William Bartram." *Phi Alpha Theta Student Journal* (1967), 12–23.
Friedrich, Otto. *Ring Lardner*. Minneapolis, 1965.
Fuchs, Daniel. *The Comic Spirit of Wallace Stevens*. Durham, N.C., 1963.
Gaskins, Avery F. "The Concept of Correspondence in the Works of Wallace Stevens and Ralph Waldo Emerson." *West Virginia University Bulletin Philological Papers*, XV (June, 1966), 62–69.
Geismar, Maxwell. *Ring Lardner and the Portrait of Folly*. New York, 1972.
―――. *Writers in Crisis: The American Novel Between Two Wars*. Boston, 1942.
Gibson, Donald B. *The Fiction of Stephen Crane*. Carbondale, 1968.
Gill, John J. "Humor in John Bartram's Journals." *American Notes and Queries*, XII (February, 1974), 90–93.
Godshalk, W. L. *In Quest of Cabell: Five Exploratory Essays*. New York, 1975.
Gordon, Armisted C., Jr. "Review of *There Were Two Pirates*," by James Branch Cabell. *New York Times Book Review*, August 11, 1946, pp. 5, 27.
Graff, Mary B. *Mandarin on the St. Johns*. Gainesville, Fla., 1953.
Grebstein, Sheldon Norman. *Hemingway's Craft*. Carbondale, 1973.
Greiner, Donald J. "Emerson, Thoreau, and Hemingway: Some Suggestions about Literary Heritage." In *Fitzgerald/Hemingway Annual*, edited by Matthew J. Bruccoli and C. E. Clark, Jr., Washington, D.C.: NCR Microcard Editions, 1971, pp. 247–61.
Guerard, Albert, Jr. "Review of *The Devil's Own Dear Son*." *New York Times*, April 17, 1949, p. 17.
Guereschi, Edward. "'The Comedian as the Letter C': Wallace Stevens' Anti-Mythological Poem." *Centennial Review*, VIII (Fall, 1964), 465–77.
Gurko, Leo. *Ernest Hemingway and the Pursuit of Heroism*. New York, 1968.
Hagemann, E. R. "'Sadder than the End': Another Look at 'The Open Boat.'" In *Stephen Crane in Transition: Centenary Essays*, edited by Joseph Katz. Dekalb, 1972.
Hall, William F. "The Continuing Relevance of Henry James' 'The American Scene.'" *Criticism*, XIII (Spring, 1971), 151–65.
Halliday, E. M. "Hemingway's Narrative Perspective." *Sewanee Review*, LX (1952), 202–18.
Hapgood, Hutchins. *A Victorian in the Modern World*. New York, 1939.
Harman, Henry E. "Sidney Lanier—A Study." *South Atlantic Quarterly*, XIV (October, 1915), 301–305.
Harris, Julia Collier, ed. *Joel Chandler Harris: Miscellaneous Literary, Political, and Social Writings*. Chapel Hill, 1931.

Hemingway, Mary Welsh. *How It Was.* New York, 1976.
"Henry James as a Literary Sphinx." *Current Literature*, XLII (June, 1907), 634-36.
Hergesheimer, Joseph. "James Branch Cabell." *American Mercury*, XIII (January, 1928), 38-47.
Hildreth, Margaret Holbrook. *Harriet Beecher Stowe: A Bibliography.* Hamden, Conn., 1976.
Hoffman, Daniel G. *The Poetry of Stephen Crane.* New York, 1957.
Hoffman, Frederick J. "Freedom and Conscious Form: Henry James and the American Self." *Virginia Quarterly Review*, XXXVII (1961), 269-85.
Holman, C. Hugh. "Ernest Hemingway." In "Modern Novelists and Contemporary American Society: A Symposium." *Shenandoah*, X (Winter, 1959), 4-11.
Holmes, Charles S. "Ring Lardner: Reluctant Artist." In *A Question of Quality: Popularity and Value in Modern Creative Writing*, edited by Louis Filler. Bowling Green, Ohio, 1976.
Holton, Milne. *Cylinder of Vision: The Fiction and Journalistic Writing of Stephen Crane.* Baton Rouge, 1972.
Hopper, Stanley Romaine. "Wallace Stevens: The Sundry Comforts of the Sun." In *Four Ways of Modern Poetry*, edited by Nathan A. Scott, Jr. Richmond, 1965.
Hovey, Richard B. *Hemingway: The Inward Terrain.* Seattle, 1968.
Howe, Irving. *Decline of the New.* New York, 1970.
———. Introduction to *The American Scene*, by Henry James. New York, 1967.
Hubbell, Jay B. *The South in American Literature: 1607-1900.* Durham, 1954.
Jackson, Blyden, and Louis D. Rubin, Jr., eds. *Black Poetry in America: Two Essays in Historical Interpretation.* Baton Rouge, 1974.
Jackson, Lena E. "Sidney Lanier in Florida." *Florida Historical Society Quarterly*, XV (October, 1936), 118-24.
Jarrell, Randall. *Poetry and the Age.* London, 1955.
Jennings, Elizabeth. *Every Changing Shape.* Philadelphia, 1962.
Kalstone, David. "Conjuring with Nature: Some Twentieth-Century Readings of Pastoral." In *Twentieth-Century Literature in Retrospect.* Harvard English Studies II, 1971.
Katz, Joseph, and Lillian B. Gilkes. "Not at Columbia: Postcards to Cora Crane." *Columbia Library Columns*, XXIII (1974), 21-30.
Katz, Joseph, ed. *Stephen Crane in Transition: Centenary Essays.* Dekalb, 1972.
Kaul, A. N. *The American Vision: Actual and Ideal Society in Nineteenth-Century Fiction.* New Haven, 1963.

Kazin, Alfred. *On Native Grounds: An Interpretation of Modern American Prose Literature.* New York, 1942.
Kennedy, Stetson. Review of *The St. Johns,* by Branch Cabell and A. J. Hanna. *New York Times Book Review,* September 5, 1943, p. 7.
Kenney, William. "Hunger and the American Dream in *To Have and Have Not.*" *CEA Critic,* XXXVI (January, 1974), 26–28.
Kermode, Frank. *Wallace Stevens.* Edinburgh, 1960.
Kern, John Dwight. *Constance Fenimore Woolson: Literary Pioneer.* Philadelphia, 1934.
Kessler, Edward. *Images of Wallace Stevens.* New Brunswick, N.J., 1972.
Knauss, James Owen. "William Pope Duval: Pioneer and State Builder." *Florida Historical Society Quarterly,* XI (January, 1933), 94–139.
Kraft, James. "On Reading *The American Scene.*" *Prose,* VI (Spring, 1973), 115–36.
Krook, Dorothea. *The Ordeal of Consciousness in Henry James.* Cambridge, 1962.
Lardner, Ring, Jr. *The Lardners: My Family Remembered.* New York, 1973.
———. "Ring Lardner and Sons: Appreciation and Assessment by a Sole Survivor." *Esquire,* VII (March, 1972), 98–103.
Laurence, Frank M. *Hemingway and the Movies.* Jackson, Miss., 1981.
Leary, Lewis. "The Forlorn Hope of Sidney Lanier." *South Atlantic Quarterly,* XLVI (1947), 263–71.
———. *Washington Irving.* Minneapolis, 1963.
Lee, B. C. "A Felicity Forever Gone: Henry James's Last Visit to America." *Bulletin of British Association for American Studies,* n.s., V (December, 1962), 31–42.
Lee, Berta Grattan. "William Bartram: Naturalist or 'Poet'?" *Early American Literature,* VII (1972–73), 124–29.
Lensing, George S. "Wallace Stevens' Letters of Rock and Water." In *Essays in Honor of Esmond Linworth Marilla,* edited by Thomas Austin Kirby and William John Olive. Baton Rouge, 1970.
Litz, A. Walton. *Introspective Voyager: The Poetic Development of Wallace Stevens.* New York, 1972.
Mackle, Elliot James, Jr. "The Eden of the South: Florida's Image in American Travel Literature and Painting, 1865–1900." Ph.D. dissertation, Emory University, 1977.
———. "Two Mistakes by Henry James in *The American Scene.*" *American Literary Realism, 1870–1910,* X (Spring, 1977), 211–12.
McCaffery, John K. M., ed. *Ernest Hemingway: The Man and His Work.* New York, 1969.
McCullough, David. "The Unexpected Mrs. Stowe." *American Heritage,* XXIV (August, 1973), 5–9, 76–80.

MacDonald, Edgar E. "Cabell's Hero: Cosmic Rebel." *Southern Literary Journal*, II (Fall, 1969), 22–42.
———. "The Glasgow-Cabell Entente." *American Literature*, XLI (March, 1969), 76–91.
———. "Glasgow, Cabell, and Richmond." *Mississippi Quarterly*, XXVII (Fall, 1974), 393–413.
McLendon, James. *Papa: Hemingway in Key West*. Miami, Fla., 1972.
Marsh, Fred T. "Mr. Cabell's 'Comedy of Conquest.'" New York *Times*, February 1, 1942, p. 6.
Marshall, Carl L. "Two Protest Poems by Albery A. Whitman." *College Language Association Journal*, XIX (September, 1975), 50–56.
Martz, Louis L. *The Poem of the Mind: Essays on Poetry/English and American*. New York, 1966.
———. "Wallace Stevens: The World as Meditation." In *Literature and Belief: English Institute Essays, 1957*, edited by M. H. Abrams. New York, 1958.
———. "The World of Wallace Stevens." In *Modern American Poetry*, edited by B. Rajan. London, 1950.
Marx, Leo. *The Machine in the Garden: Technology and the Pastoral Ideal in America*. New York, 1964.
Mason, Julian. "Black Writers of the South." *Mississippi Quarterly*, XXXI (Spring, 1978), 169–83.
Mattfield, Mary S. "Journey to the Wilderness: Two Travelers in Florida, 1696–1774." *Florida Historical Quarterly*, XLV (April, 1967), 327–51.
Medeiros, Patricia M. "Three Travelers: Carver, Bartram, and Woolman." In *American Literature, 1764–1789: The Revolutionary Years*, edited by Everett Emerson. Madison, 1977.
Michaud, Regis. *Emerson: The Enraptured Yankee*. Translated by George Boas. New York, 1930.
Millett, Fred B. "James Branch Cabell." In *Minor American Novelists*, edited by Charles Alva Hoyt. Carbondale, 1970.
Mills, Ralph J., Jr. *Contemporary American Poetry*. New York, 1965.
Moore, Rayburn S. *Constance F. Woolson*. New Haven, 1963.
———. "The Strange Irregular Rhythm of Life: James's Late Tales and Constance Woolson." *South Atlantic Bulletin*, XLI (1976), 86–93.
Morris, Wright. "Henry James's *The American Scene*." *Texas Quarterly*, I (Summer–Autumn, 1958), 27–42.
———. *The Territory Ahead*. New York, 1957.
Morse, Samuel French. *Wallace Stevens: Poetry as Life*. New York, 1970.
Mulqueen, James E. "A Reading of Wallace Stevens' 'The Comedian as the Letter C.'" *Cimarron Review*, XIII (October, 1970), 35–42.

Murphy, Francis. "The Comedian as the Letter C." *Wisconsin Studies in Contemporary Literature*, III (Spring-Summer, 1962), 79-99.
Nagel, James. "Stephen Crane's 'The Clan of No-Name.'" *Kyusha American Literature*, XIV (1972), 34-42.
Nahal, Chaman. *The Narrative Pattern in Ernest Hemingway's Fiction.* Rutherford, 1971.
Nassar, Eugene Paul. *Wallace Stevens: An Anatomy of Figuration.* Philadelphia, 1965.
Ober, Frederick A. *Ferdinand De Soto and the Invasion of Florida.* New York, 1906.
O'Brien, Edward J. *The Best Short Stories of 1926 and the Yearbook of the American Short Story.* New York, 1927.
O'Connor, Richard. *Ernest Hemingway.* New York, 1971.
Olschki, Leonardo. "Ponce de Leon's Fountain of Youth: History of a Geographical Myth." *Hispanic American Historical Review*, XXI (August, 1941), 361-85.
Osborn, Neal J. "The Riddle in 'The Clan': A Key to Crane's Major Fiction?" *Bulletin of the New York Times Public Library*, LXIX (April, 1965), 247-58.
Parks, Edd Winfield. "James Branch Cabell." In *Southern Renascence: The Literature of the Modern South*, edited by Louis D. Rubin, Jr., and Robert D. Jacobs. Baltimore, 1953.
———. "James Branch Cabell." *Mississippi Quarterly*, XX (Spring, 1967), 97-102.
———. *Sidney Lanier: The Man, the Poet, the Critic.* Athens, Ga., 1968.
Patrick, Walton R. *Ring Lardner.* New York, 1963.
Pattee, Fred Lewis. "Constance Fenimore Woolson and the South." *South Atlantic Quarterly*, XXXVIII (April, 1939), 130-41.
Pauly, Thomas H. "The Literary Sketch in Nineteenth-Century America." *Texas Studies in Literature and Language*, XVII (Summer, 1975), 489-503.
Pearce, Roy Harvey, and J. Hillis Miller, eds. *The Act of the Mind: Essays on the Poetry of Wallace Stevens.* Baltimore, 1965.
Pearsall, Robert Brainard. *The Life and Writings of Ernest Hemingway.* Amsterdam, 1973.
Perlis, Alan. *Wallace Stevens: A World of Transforming Shapes.* Lewisburg, Pa., 1976.
Peters, Emmett, Jr. "Cabell: The Making of A Rebel." *Carolina Quarterly*, XIV (Spring, 1962), 74-82.
Phelps, Donald. "Shut Up, He Explained." *Shenandoah*, XXIX (Summer, 1978), 84-100.

Phillips, Gene D. *Hemingway and Film.* New York, 1980.
Pinkerton, Jan. "Wallace Stevens in the Tropics: A Conservative Protest." *Yale Review*, LX (December, 1970), 215–27.
Pizer, Donald. "Stephen Crane: A Review of Scholarship and Criticism Since 1969." *Studies in the Novel*, X (Spring, 1978), 120–45.
Pritchett, V. S. "The Traveller Returns." *New Statesman*, February 21, 1969, pp. 259–60.
Randel, William. "The Cook in 'The Open Boat.'" *American Literature*, XXXIV (November, 1962), 405–11.
———. "From Slate to Emerald Green: More Light on Crane's Jacksonville Visit." *Nineteenth-Century Fiction*, XIX (March, 1965), 357–68.
———. "Stephen Crane's Jacksonville." *South Atlantic Quarterly*, LXII (Spring, 1963), 268–74.
Rascoe, Burton. "Cabell, Unorthodox as Always: An Old Master of the Deft Barb Completes His Florida Trilogy." *New York Herald Tribune Weekly Book Review*, April 17, 1949, p. 4.
Redman, Ben Ray. "Cabell. . . ." *Saturday Review of Literature*, February 7, 1942, p. 7.
———. "A True 'Comedy of Diversion.'" *Saturday Review of Literature*, August 10, 1946, pp. 7–8.
Rees, Robert A., and Earl N. Harbert, eds. *Fifteen American Authors Before 1900.* Madison, 1971.
Review of *The Devil's Own Dear Son*, by James Branch Cabell. *New Yorker*, May 7, 1949, pp. 109–10.
[Y.Y.] Review of *The American Scene*, by Henry James. *Bookman*, XXXI (March, 1907), 265–66.
Review of *Palmetto-Leaves*, by Harriet Beecher Stowe. *Overland Monthly*, X (June, 1873), 583–84.
Ribaut, Jean. *The Whole and True Discouerye of Terra Florida.* A facsimile reprint of the London edition of 1563; Gainesville, Fla., 1964.
Richardson, Lyon N. "Constance Fenimore Woolson, 'Novelist Laureate' of America." *South Atlantic Quarterly*, XXXIX (January, 1940), 18–36.
Richmond, Mrs. Henry L. "Ralph Waldo Emerson in Florida . . . And Emerson's Largely Unpublished Little Journal At St. Augustine January–March 1827." *Florida Historical Quarterly*, XVIII (October, 1939), 74–93.
Riddel, Joseph N. *The Clairvoyant Eye: The Poetry and Poetics of Wallace Stevens.* Baton Rouge, 1965.
———. "Stevens on Imagination—The Point of Departure." in *The Quest for Imagination: Essays In Twentieth-Century Aesthetic Criticism*, edited by O. B. Hardison, Jr. Cleveland, 1971.

Rogers, Benjamin F. "Florida Seen Through the Eyes of Nineteenth Century Travellers." *Florida Historical Quarterly*, XXXIX (October, 1955), 177–89.
Rosmond, Babette, and Henry Morgan, eds. *Shut Up, He Explained: A Ring Lardner Selection*. New York, 1962.
Ross, Lillian. *Portrait of Hemingway*. New York, 1961.
Rothman, William. "To Have and Have Not Adapted a Novel." In *The Modern American Novel and the Movies*, edited by Gerald Peary and Roger Schatzkin. New York, 1978.
Rourke, Constance. *American Humor: A Study of the National Character*. 1931; rpr. Garden City, N.Y., 1953.
Rovit, Earl. *Ernest Hemingway*. New York, 1963.
Rubin, Louis D., Jr., ed. *The Comic Imagination in American Literature*. New Brunswick, 1973.
Rubin, Louis D., Jr. "James Branch Cabell Today." Baltimore *Evening Sun*, July 6, 1956, 20.
———. *No Place on Earth: Ellen Glasgow, James Branch Cabell, and Richmond-in-Virginia*. Austin, 1959.
———. "The Self Recaptured." *Kenyon Review*, XXV (1963), 393–415.
———, ed. *The Literary South*. New York, 1979.
Rubenstein, Annette T. "Henry James, American Novelist or: Isabel Archer, Emerson's Grand-daughter." In *Weapons of Criticism: Marxism in America and the Literary Tradition*, edited by Norman Rudich. Palo Alto, 1976.
Rusk, Ralph L. *The Life of Ralph Waldo Emerson*. New York, 1949.
Russell, Phillips. *Emerson: The Wisest American*. New York, 1929.
Ryan, William James. "Uses of Irony in *To Have and Have Not*." *Modern Fiction Studies*, XIV (Autumn, 1968), 329–36.
Schlegel, Dorothy B. "James Branch Cabell and Southern Romanticism." In *Southern Writers: Appraisals in Our Time*, edited by R. C. Simonini. Essay Index Reprint Series. Freeport, N.Y., 1969.
———. *James Branch Cabell: The Richmond Iconoclast*. New York, 1975.
Shaw, Samuel. *Ernest Hemingway*. New York, 1973.
Sherman, Joan R. "Albery Allson Whitman: Poet of Beauty and Manliness." *College Language Association Journal*, XV (December, 1971), 126–43.
———. *Invisible Poets: Afro-Americans of the Nineteenth Century*. Urbana, 1974.
Shourds, Raymond. "Hemingway's Key West Home." *Mainliner*, XIII (April, 1969), 14–17.
Shulman, Robert. "Community, Perception, and the Development of

Stephen Crane: From *The Red Badge* to 'The Open Boat.' *American Literature*, L (November, 1978), 441–60.
Silver, Bruce. "William Bartram's and Other Eighteenth-Century Accounts of Nature." *Journal of the History of Ideas*, XXXIX (1978), 597–614.
Simons, Hi. " 'The Comedian as the Letter C': Its Sense and Its Significance." In *The Achievement of Wallace Stevens*, edited by Ashley Brown and Robert S. Waller. Philadelphia, 1962.
Smiley, Nixon. "Not a Town, Not Even a Village." *Miami Herald Sunday Magazine*, April 23, 1967, p. 10.
Smith, Carl S. "James's Travels, Travel Writings, and the Development of His Art." *Modern Language Quarterly*, XXXVIII (December, 1977), 367–80.
Solomon, Eric. *Stephen Crane: From Parody to Realism*. Cambridge, 1966.
Staebler, Warren. *Ralph Waldo Emerson*. New York, 1973.
Stallman, R. W. "Journalist Crane in that Dinghy." *Bulletin of the New York Public Library*, LXXII (April, 1968), 261–77.
———. *Stephen Crane: A Biography*. Rev. ed. New York, 1973.
Stallman, R. W., and Lillian Gilkes, eds., *Stephen Crane: Letters*. New York, 1960.
Starke, Aubrey. "Sidney Lanier: Man of Science in the Field of Letters." *American Scholar*, II (1933), 389–408.
Stephens, Robert O., ed. *Ernest Hemingway: The Critical Reception*. New York, 1977.
Stern, Herbert J. *Wallace Stevens: Art of Uncertainty*. Ann Arbor, 1966.
Sterner, D. W. "Henry James and the Idea of Culture in 'The American Scene.' " *Modern Age*, XVIII (Summer, 1974), 283–90.
Stevens, A. Wilber. "Henry James' *The American Scene*: The Vision of Value." *Twentieth Century Literature*, I (April, 1955), 27–33.
Stevens, Holly. *Souvenirs and Prophecies: The Young Wallace Stevens*. New York, 1977.
Tarrant, Desmond. *James Branch Cabell: The Dream and the Reality*. Norman, 1967.
Tebeau, Charlton W. *A History of Florida*. Rev. ed. Coral Gables, Fla., 1980.
Tindall, George Brown. *The Emergence of the New South, 1913–1945*. Baton Rouge, 1967. Vol. X of *A History of the South*, edited by Wendell Holmes Stephenson and E. Merton Coulter. 10 vols.
Tindall, William York. *Wallace Stevens*. Minneapolis, 1961.
Trachtenberg, Alan. "The American Scene: Versions of the City." *Massachusetts Review*, VIII (Spring, 1967), 281–95.
———. "The Craft of Vision." *Critique*, IV (Winter, 1961–62), 41–55.

Untermeyer, Louis. *James Branch Cabell: The Man and His Masks*. Richmond, 1970.
Van Doren, Carl. *James Branch Cabell*. New York, 1932.
Vendler, Helen Hennessy. *On Extended Wings: Wallace Stevens' Longer Poems*. Cambridge, 1969.
Wagenknecht, Edward. *Cavalcade of the American Novel*. New York, 1952.
———. *Harriet Beecher Stowe: The Known and the Unknown*. New York, 1965.
———, ed. *The Letters of James Branch Cabell*. Norman, 1975.
Waldhorn, Arthur. *A Reader's Guide to Ernest Hemingway*. New York, 1972.
Ward, J. A. "Henry James's America: Versions of Oppression." *Mississippi Quarterly*, XIII (1960), 30–44.
Warfel, Harry R. *American Novelists Today*. New York, 1951.
Warren, Robert Penn. "The Blind Poet: Sidney Lanier." *American Review*, II (March, 1934), 27–45.
———. "Ernest Hemingway." In *Critiques and Essays on Modern Fiction: 1920–1951*, edited by John W. Aldridge. New York, 1952.
———. "Novelist—Philosophers—X: Hemingway." *Horizon*, XV (1947), 156–80.
Watkins, Floyd C. *The Flesh and the World: Eliot, Hemingway, Faulkner*. Nashville, 1971.
Wegelin, Christof. *The Image of Europe in Henry James*. Dallas, 1958.
Weir, Sybil B. "Southern Womanhood in the Novels of Constance Fenimore Woolson." *Mississippi Quarterly*, XXIX (1976), 559–68.
Wells, Arvin R. *Jesting Moses: A Study in Cabellian Comedy*. Gainesville, Fla., 1962.
Weston, Susan B. *Wallace Stevens: An Introduction to the Poetry*. New York, 1977.
White, William, ed. *By-Line: Ernest Hemingway: Selected Articles and Dispatches of Four Decades*. New York, 1967.
———. *Guide to Ernest Hemingway*. Columbus, Ohio, 1969.
Williams, Stanley T. *The Life of Washington Irving*. 2 vols. New York, 1935.
Wilson, Edmund. *The Bit Between My Teeth: A Literary Chronicle of 1950–1965*. New York, 1965.
———. *A Literary Chronicle: 1920–1950*. Garden City, N.Y., 1956.
Wilson, Forrest. *Crusader in Crinoline: The Life of Harriet Beecher Stowe*. Philadelphia, 1941.
Woodward, C. Vann. *The Burden of Southern History*. Rev. ed. Baton Rouge, 1968.
———. *Origins of the New South, 1877–1913*. Baton Rouge, 1971. Vol. IX

of *A History of the South*, edited by Wendell Holmes Stephenson and E. Merton Coulter. 10 vols.

Wright, Richard. *White Man, Listen!* 1957; rpr. Garden City, N.Y., 1964.

Wylder, Delbert E. *Hemingway's Heroes*. Albuquerque, 1969.

Yardley, Jonathan. *Ring: A Biography of Ring Lardner*. New York, 1977.

Young, Philip. *Ernest Hemingway*. New York, 1952.

———. "Focus on *To Have and Have Not*: To Have Not: Tough Luck." In *Tough Guy Writers of the Thirties*, edited by David Madden. Carbondale, 1968.

Index

Auden, W. H., 57
Automobiles: impact of, on Florida development, 78

Baker, Carlos, 99, 100, 104–105
Bartram, John, 1, 8
Bartram, William, 1–4, 13, 19, 23, 24, 42, 111, 112, 126, 138; and artistic imagination in Florida, 4; Cabell on, 117; influence of, on Irving, 16, 17–18
— *Travels*, 1–4
Baskin, Norton, 112
Beer, Thomas, 47
Belleair: and Ring Lardner, 82, 85, 86, 88
Benedict, Clare, 38
Benét, Stephen Vincent, 115
Bigelow, Gordon, 108, 111–12
Bishop, Elizabeth, 138
Blacks: in Florida, 20, 22, 29, 30. *See also* Slavery
Broward, Napoleon B., 45, 78
Buitenhuis, Peter, 57

Cabell, James Branch, 9, 112–23; and Bartram, 117; and Rawlings, 112, 113, 116; treatment of Florida in work of, 112, 113, 114–15, 120, 122–23
— works of: *The Biography of Manuel*, 114; *The Devil's Own Dear Son*, 115, 120–22; *It Happened in Florida*, 112, 114; *Jurgen*, 113, 114, 115, 120, 122; *The St. Johns*, 115–19
Cabot, John, 6
Civil War, 22, 28, 29, 30, 34, 43, 44; in Florida, 26–27, 45
Collins, John S., 78, 79
Conrad, Joseph, 55
Coral Gables: development of, 79
Crane, Cora Taylor (Mrs. Stephen), 48–49, 118
Crane, Stephen, 44–55, 57, 58, 95, 118; background of, 46; in Florida, 5, 44, 46, 47, 48; treatment of Florida in work of, 51, 55, 64–65
— works of: "The Clan of No-Name," 49, 54–55; "Flanagan and His Short

Filibustering Adventure," 52–54, 55; "The Open Boat," 5, 48, 49–51, 52, 53, 55, 95
Crews, Harry, 138
Cross Creek, 108
Cuba: ties of, with Florida, 45, 47, 48

Davis, Joe Lee, 114
Davis, Richard Harding, 46
Daytona Beach, 48, 51
Depression of 1930s: and Florida, 79, 80, 93, 94
De Soto, Hernando, 7, 36
Dickinson, Jonathan, 8
Disney World, 138
Dos Passos, John, 96
Dovell, J. E., 8, 27, 79
Durham, Frank, 113
DuVal, William Pope, 16, 17, 24; as inspiration for Irving, 17–20

Edel, Leon, 56, 58
Eden: Florida as image of, 3, 4, 9–10, 20, 22, 23, 24, 56, 91; in Bartram's *Travels*, 3, 24; in Irving's "Seminoles," 20; to Rawlings, 109; to Stowe, 29, 30; to Whitman, 20, 22, 23–25; to Woolson, 41, 42
Elder, Donald, 85
Elderly: Florida as mecca for, 78, 79, 86
Emerson, Ralph Waldo, 9, 11–15, 32; in Florida, 4–5, 11–15, 64; vision of Florida of, 12, 13, 14, 15
—works of: "St. Augustine," 5, 13; "Society and Solitude," 15
England: dominion of, over Florida, 8–9, 45
Epcot Center, 138
Evans, Elizabeth, 82
Everglades, 16, 78

Fadiman, Clifton, 87
Filibusters: and Florida, 45, 48, 51
Flagler, Henry, 27, 93, 96, 118
Florida: acquisition of, by U.S., 9; development of, 5, 6, 15, 64, 78, 79–80, 83, 94, 138; discovery of, 6–7, 8; exploration of, 2, 7, 8, 15; history of, as source of literary inspiration, 38, 113, 114, 123; population of, 6, 79, 138; present conditions in, 6, 138; as symbol of American life, 90, 95–96
Florida Keys: development of, in 1930s, 94. *See also* Key West
Ford, Jesse Hill, 138
Fothergill, Dr. John, 2
Fountain of Youth: myth of, 7
France: claim of, to Florida, 8
Frederic, Harold, 55

Geismar, Maxwell, 83–84
Glasgow, Ellen, 113
Gold Coast (Miami), 47, 58
Gurko, Leo, 104, 106

Hanna, A. J., 115, 116, 118, 119. *See also* Cabell, James Branch—works of: *The St. Johns*
Hemingway, Ernest, 9, 92–106, 107; and Crane, 95; image of Florida in work of, 6, 93, 96–97, 98, 101, 105, 106; and James, 95; in Key West, 5–6, 92–98, 105–106; and Lardner, 95
—works of: *A Farewell to Arms*, 106; *To Have and Have Not*, 95, 98–105, 106; *Islands in the Stream*, 106; *The Old Man and the Sea*, 106; "The Three-Day Blow," 94
Hemingway, Pauline Pfeiffer (Mrs. Ernest), 92, 96, 97
Hoffman, Frederick, 57
Holman, Hugh, 95
Howells, William Dean, 39
Hubbell, Jay B., 14
Hurricanes: impact of, on Florida, 79, 83, 94

Indians: in Florida, 9, 15
Indian wars: in Florida, 15, 16; literary responses to, 15, 16–20, 22–23, 36
Invalids: Florida as haven for, 15, 32, 36, 37, 58
Irving, Washington, 16–20, 24, 25; and Bartram's *Travels*, 17–18; and Florida Indian wars, 16–20; vision of Florida of, 17, 20

—works of: "The Seminoles," 17–19; *Wolfert's Roost*, 17

Jackson, Andrew, 9, 16
Jacksonville, 47, 48, 49, 58; and Crane, 44, 46, 47, 48; James on, 59–60; King on, 31; Lanier on, 35–36; and Spanish-American War, 46
James, Henry, 9, 24, 41, 55–65, 80, 83, 88, 95, 96, 117, 138; compared with Hemingway, 95–96; on Florida, 5, 59, 60, 61, 85, 134; Florida tour of, 56, 58–59; image of Florida in work of, 56, 59, 62–63, 64–65; Palm Beach sketches of, 77–78, 85; return of, to America (1904), 55; and Woolson, 38, 39
—works of: *The American Scene*, 56–65; "Daisy Miller," 61
Jarrell, Randall, 126

Kazin, Alfred, 96–97, 98, 99
Key West, 5–6, 45, 46, 49, 93–94, 96–97, 98, 106, 107; Dos Passos on, 96; Hemingway in, 5–6, 92–93, 101, 105, 106; Hemingway on, 5–6; Stevens on, 124–25
King, Edward, 30–33, 42, 43, 49, 57; in Florida, 31–33; vision of Florida of, 31–32, 33
—*The Great South*, 31–33, 36

Land boom: in Florida (1920s), 5, 78, 79–80, 83
Landscape, American: artistic interpretations of, 1–2
Lanier, Sidney, 33–37, 42, 43, 58; background of, 34; Cabell on, 117; in Florida, 33–35, 37; on Indian wars 36; poems of, about Florida, 37
—works of: *Florida: Its Scenery, Climate, and History*, 34–37; *Sunrise*, 37
Lardner, Ellis Abbott (Mrs. Ring), 80, 82
Lardner, Ring, 9, 61, 77–91, 95, 98; background of, 80–82; and baseball scandals of 1920s, 81–82; in Florida, 5, 77, 82; image of Florida in writing of, 5, 78, 83, 85, 86, 90, 91; style of, 82

—works of: "The Golden Honeymoon," 83, 85, 86–89, 90; "Gullible's Travels," 83–85, 86, 90; "Sun Cured," 83, 89–90
Lehan, Richard, 105
Levenson, J. C., 51
Local-color fiction, 20, 22, 31, 39; Florida as setting for, 37–38; and Woolson, 37–38, 39, 41, 42
Long, Ray, 85–86
Lorimer, George Horace, 85

McLendon, James, 94, 96
Mandarin: Stowe at, 29, 30, 32, 125
Matanzas, Battle of, 8
Mencken, H. L., 88
Menéndez, Pedro, 8
Merrick, George E., 79
Miami, 47, 78, 79, 89, 90, 125
Midnight Cowboy, 138
Morse, Samuel French, 125
Mosquito Inlet, 49, 51
Mt. Cornelia, 118
Murat, Achille, 14–15

Natural Bridge, Battle of, 27
New Deal: and Florida Keys, 94

Oklawaha River, 15, 27, 33, 35, 36
Olustee, Battle of, 26
Overseas Highway, 94, 96, 105

Palatka, 27, 33
Palm Beach, 47, 58, 59, 64, 77, 78, 79, 83, 84, 90; James on, 60–62; as setting of Lardner's "Gullible's Travels," 85
Patrick, Walton, 82
Pinkerton, Jan, 126–27
Plant, Henry, 27, 118
Ponce de León, Juan, 7, 9, 33, 89, 108
Powell, Judge Arthur, 125

Railroads: construction of, in Florida, 6, 27, 28, 34, 47, 58, 93, 94, 96, 118
Randel, William, 47
Rascoe, Burton, 116, 118
Rawlings, Charles, 107–108
Rawlings, Marjorie Kinnan, 107–112; background of, 107–108; and Cabell,

112, 113, 116; at Cross Creek, 107, 108; and Stevens, 132; treatment of Florida in writing of, 108, 109, 111, 112
—works of: "Cracker Chidlings," 108; *Cross Creek*, 109–112, 132; *The Golden Apples*, 108; *The Sojourner*, 109; *South Moon Under*, 108; *When the Whippoorwill*, 108; *The Yearling*, 108, 109
Reconciliation fiction, 22, 25, 40, 43; Florida as image in, 43. *See also* Local-color fiction
Reconstruction: Florida during, 27
Revolution, American: and Florida, 8–9
Ribault, Jean, 7–8, 117
Rice, Grantland, 82
Riddel, Joseph N., 129
Roads: construction of, in Florida, 78
Rubin, Louis D., Jr., 95, 114, 115

St. Augustine, 8, 58, 59, 117, 120; and Cabell, 112, 113, 114, 115–19, 121, 122; and Emerson, 11, 12, 13, 14, 64; and James, 58, 62; and King, 32–33; and Woolson, 39
St. Johns River, 2, 4, 5, 15, 29, 30, 48, 50, 118; and Bartram, 2–4, 8; and Cabell, 115–19; and James, 59; and King, 32, 33; and Rawlings, 111; and Stowe, 5, 29, 30
St. Petersburg, 79, 90; and Lardner, 82, 85, 86, 88
Schwartz, Delmore, 98–99
Scribner's Monthly Magazine, 30, 33, 108
Seminole wars. *See* Indian wars
Sherman, Joan, 21, 22
Silver Springs, 31, 33, 35
Slavery: in Florida, 20, 28; images of, in works of Whitman, 22, 23. *See also* Blacks
Spain: dominion of, over Florida, 8, 9, 36
Spanish-American War: and Florida, 45–46; and Crane, 49
Steamboats: and development of Florida, 15

Stern, Herbert, 128
Stevens, Wallace, 9, 42, 124–36; on Florida, 4, 6, 124–25, 132; image of Florida in poetry of, 6, 125–27, 128, 130, 133, 134, 136, 137; visits of, to Florida, 124, 125, 126
—works of: "The Comedian as the Letter C," 128–29; "Fabliau of Florida," 128; "Farewell to Florida," 128, 132–33; "O Florida, Venereal Soil," 129–30; *Harmonium*, 126, 127, 128, 129, 132; *Ideas of Order*, 126, 127–28, 132; "The Idea of Order at Key West," 127–28, 134–36; "Indian River," 131–32; "Nomad Exquisite," 130–31; *Parts of a World*, 126; "Sailing After Lunch," 132; "Sunday Morning," 128, 130, 131
Stowe, Harriet Beecher, 6, 28–30, 32, 42, 43, 125; and Cabell, 117–18; in Florida, 5, 21–22, 29, 30; praise of Florida by, 28–30; and Whitman, 21
—works of: *Palmetto-Leaves*, 29–30; *Uncle Tom's Cabin*, 21, 28, 29, 118

Tallahassee, 14, 27
Tampa, 45, 46, 49, 94, 120
Tarpon Springs, 94
Thoreau, Henry David, 108, 110
Tourism: in Florida, 24, 31, 32, 49, 58, 78–79, 80, 94; and Civil War, 27; in Jacksonville, 47; in Key West, 94; in St. Augustine, 113; and World War II, 137
Trammel, Park, 78

Van Doren, Carl, 113
Vespucci, Amerigo, 6

Waterways: development of, in Florida, 27, 28
Whitman, Albery, 20–25; background of, 20–21; analysis of work of, 21–25; and Stowe, 21; vision of Florida in work of, 20, 22, 23–25
—*Twasinta's Seminoles, or the Rape of Florida*, 20, 22–24
Williams, Stanley, 18
Wilson, Edmund, 91

Woolson, Constance Fenimore, 37–43; background of, 38; image of Florida in fiction of, 37–38, 39–41, 42; and local-color fiction, 37–38, 39, 41, 42; and reconciliation fiction, 40
—works of: *Castle Nowhere*, 39; *East Angels*, 39–42; *For the Major*, 39; *Rodman the Keeper*, 39

World War I, 81; and Florida, 79, 93
World War II: and Florida, 137
Wright, Richard, 21

Yardley, Jonathan, 80, 88
Young, Philip, 95, 104